Puffin Books
The Puffin Junior Dictionary

This dictionary is intended primarily for seven- to nine-year-olds. It contains approximately 4,800 headwords and over 300 additional items in supplementary lists. All the headwords are defined simply and clearly in terms of a vocabulary of less than 2,000 words. Each sense of a word is numbered separately and begins on a fresh line.

The words chosen for inclusion are those most likely to be needed by children in this age-range. Accordingly, irregular or difficult plural and verbal forms have been included, while very easy words, such as *at*, *but*, *cat*, *it*, and so on, have been omitted.

Examples of usage are provided wherever appropriate and printed in italics.

Simple pronunciation guides are given for words with difficult or ambiguous pronunciations.

The names of days, months, numbers, shapes, colours, planets, continents, peoples and places are listed separately at the end of the book, but some are also included in the body of the dictionary.

The Puffin Junior Dictionary

Compiled by Rosemary Sansome

Illustrated by Susan Shields

Puffin Books

by arrangement with Oxford University Press

Puffin Books, Penguin Books Ltd, Harmondsworth, Middlesex, England
Viking Penguin Inc., 40 West 23rd Street, New York, New York 10010, U.S.A.
Penguin Books Australia Ltd, Ringwood, Victoria, Australia
Penguin Books Canada Ltd, 2801 John Street, Markham, Ontario, Canada L3R 1B4
Penguin Books (N.Z.) Ltd, 182–190 Wairau Road, Auckland 10, New Zealand

First published by Oxford University Press 1978
Published in Puffin Books 1982
Reprinted 1983 (twice), 1985

Copyright © Oxford University Press, 1978
Illustrations copyright © Susan Shields, 1982
All rights reserved

Made and printed in Great Britain by
Hazell Watson and Viney Ltd, Aylesbury
Composition in Helvetica by
Filmtype Services Limited, Scarborough, North Yorkshire
Designed by Peter Ward

Aa

abandon **1** to leave for ever
Abandon ship!
2 to give up
Abandon all hope of rescue!

abbey **1** a big, old church once used by monks or nuns
Westminster Abbey
2 a place where monks or nuns live and work

abbreviation a short way of writing a word or a group of words
P.T.O. is an abbreviation for please turn over.

ability the power to do something

able having the power to do something

aboard on a ship, bus, train, or aeroplane
All aboard!

about **1** just before or just after
It's about four o'clock.
2 having to do with
a book about ships

above **1** overhead
the sky above
2 higher than
The aeroplane flew above the clouds.

abroad in another country
a holiday abroad

abrupt sudden
an abrupt ending

absent not here

accelerator one of the pedals in a car. The driver presses it with his foot to make the car go faster.

accent the way people say their words
Australians have a different accent from Americans.

accept to take what is offered to you

accident **1** something bad that happens and is not meant to happen
2 by accident by chance
We met by accident.

accompany **1** to go with someone
2 to play the piano while someone sings or dances

account **1** a story about something that has happened
2 a list that tells you how much money you owe or have spent

accurate correct and exact

accuse to say that a certain person has done something wrong

5

ace a card used in games, marked to show it is number one. A pack of cards has four aces in it.

ache to have a pain that goes on hurting
*My head is **aching**.*

achievement something difficult or special that you have done

acid a kind of liquid that tastes sour and can sometimes burn your skin. Lemons contain a very weak acid.

acorn the nut of an oak tree

acrobat someone who does exciting jumping and balancing tricks to entertain people

across from one side to the other

*I swam **across** the river.*

act 1 to take part in a play 2 to do something

action 1 doing something 2 something that is done

active busy or working

activity 1 being busy doing things 2 something for you to do

actor a man who acts in a play

actress a woman who acts in a play

actual real

add 1 to put with something else to make it bigger 2 to find the answer to a sum like this $3 + 3 =$

adder a small snake with poisonous teeth

addition 1 adding numbers 2 something that is added

additional extra

address the number of the house and the names of the street and town where someone lives

adjective any word that tells you what someone or something is like.
Beautiful, tall, nasty, delicious, and *difficult* are all adjectives.

admiral a very important officer in the navy

admire 1 to think someone or something is very good
*The teacher **admired** his work.*
2 to look at something and enjoy it
*They were **admiring** the view.*

admission letting someone in

admit 1 to let someone come in
2 to say you were the person who did something, when someone asks if you did it
*He **admitted** that he stole the jewels.*

adopt to take someone into your family as your own child

adore to like very much

adult someone who is fully grown

advance to move forward

advantage anything that helps you to do better than other people
*an unfair **advantage***

adventure something exciting that happens to you

adverb any word that tells you how, when, or where something happens.
Away, often, somewhere, now, slowly, and *quickly* are all adverbs.

advertisement (*say* ad-ver-tis-ment)
words or pictures that try to make you buy something

advice something said to someone to help him decide what to do

advise to tell someone what you think it would be best for him to do

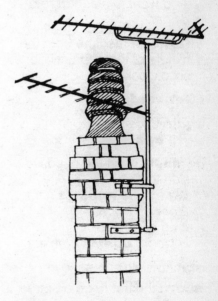

aerial wires or metal rods for picking up or sending out radio and television programmes

aeroplane a flying machine with wings and an engine

affect to make someone different in some way

affection a feeling you have for someone or something you like a lot

afford to have enough money to pay for something

afraid frightened

after **1** later than
*You finished **after** me.*
2 following
*Dad went to sleep **after** dinner.*

afternoon the time from the middle of the day until about six o'clock

afterwards later

again once more
*Try **again**!*

against **1** on the opposite side to
*We played **against** your team and won.*
2 on or next to
*He leant **against** the wall.*

age how old someone or something is

agent someone whose job is to arrange things for people
*a travel **agent***

agile able to move quickly and easily

agree to think the same as someone else

aground trapped on sand or rocks in shallow water. Ships sometimes run aground on rocks and are badly damaged.

ahead in front
*I went on **ahead** to open the gate.*

aid **1** help
2 something that helps
*a hearing **aid***

aim **1** to point a gun at something
2 to throw, kick, or shoot at something you are trying to hit
3 to try to do something
*They **aimed** at finishing in time for tea.*

air what everyone breathes

aircraft any aeroplane or helicopter
*two **aircraft***

air force a group of people trained to use aeroplanes for fighting

air-gun a gun that uses air instead of an explosive to make the bullets shoot out

air-hostess a woman whose job is to look after people travelling in an aeroplane

airport a place where people can get on or off aeroplanes

air-tight tightly closed so that air cannot get into it or out of it
an **air-tight** jar

aisle (*say* ile *to rhyme with* tile)
a path between groups of seats. Churches, cinemas, aeroplanes, and buses have aisles.

alarm **1** a sudden, frightened feeling
2 a warning sound or sign

album a book where you can keep things like stamps or photographs

alert lively and ready for anything
an **alert** policeman

alight on fire

alive living

all **1** everyone or everything
Let's start singing. **All** together now ...
2 the whole of something
He's eaten **all** the cake.

alley a very narrow street

alligator a large animal that lives in rivers in America and China. It has short legs, a long body, and sharp teeth.

allotment a small piece of land that you can pay to use. People grow vegetables, fruit, and flowers on their allotments.

allow to let something happen

all right **1** safe and well
2 I agree
All right, you can stay up.

ally a person or country fighting on the same side

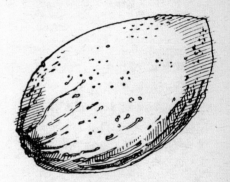

almond a kind of flat nut with a very hard shell

almost very nearly
We're **almost** home now.

alone by yourself or by itself

along **1** from one end to the other
He ran **along** the top of the wall.
2 **Come along**! Hurry up!

aloud in a voice that can be heard

alphabet all the letters used in writing a language, arranged in order

already **1** by this time
*He was **already** there when we arrived.*
2 before now
*I've **already** done that.*

Alsatian a kind of big, strong dog

also as well
*jelly and **also** ice-cream*

altar the table with a cross on it in a church

alter to change

alteration a change in someone or something

although though
***Although** it was hot, she wore a fur coat.*

altogether counting everything or everyone
*There are twenty-nine in our class **altogether**.*

aluminium a very light metal, coloured like silver

always at all times
*He's **always** hungry.*

amateur **1** someone who does something as a hobby
2 someone who takes part in a sport and is not paid

amaze to surprise greatly

ambition something that you want to do very much
*Her **ambition** is to be a doctor.*

ambulance a van for taking injured or ill people to hospital

ammunition anything that is fired from a gun

among in the middle of
*Your book must be somewhere **among** these.*

amount how much or how many there are
*a large **amount** of money*

amuse **1** to make someone laugh or smile
2 to make time pass pleasantly for someone
*I was **amusing** myself with this puzzle.*

amusement **1** an amused feeling
2 something that entertains you

ancestor a member of the same family who lived long ago

anchor (*say* anker)
a heavy metal hook joined to a ship by a chain. It is dropped into the sea, where it digs into the bottom to keep the ship still.

anchor

ancient very old

angel a messenger sent by God

anger a strong feeling that you get when you are not pleased. It makes you want to fight or hurt someone.

angle the corner where two lines meet (see page 249)

angler a fisherman who uses a rod, hook, and line

angry feeling anger

animal anything that lives and can move about. Birds, fish, snakes, wasps, and elephants are all animals.

ankle the thin part of the leg where it is joined to the foot

anniversary a day when you remember something special that happened on the same day in another year
*a wedding **anniversary***

announce to say something in front of a lot of people

annoy to make someone angry

annual **1** a book that comes out once a year
2 happening every year
*an **annual** meeting*

anorak a waterproof jacket with a hood

another **1** a different one
2 one more
*No, you can't have **another** cake.*

answer **1** to say something to someone who has asked you a question
2 something that is said or done in return

ant a tiny insect

Antarctic the very cold land in the south of the world

antelope a wild animal that looks like a deer. Antelope are found in Africa and parts of Asia.

11

antique (*say* an-teek)
something valuable that is
very old

anxious worried

any **1** one or some
*Have you **any** wool?*
2 at all
*Are you **any** better?*

anybody, anyone any
person

anything any thing
*It's so dark, I can't see
anything.*

anywhere in any place

apart away from each other
*London and Sydney are far
apart.*

ape an animal like a large
monkey with long arms and
no tail. Chimpanzees and
gorillas are apes.

apologize to say that you are
sorry for doing something
wrong
*He keeps **apologizing**.*

apparatus special things that
you use for doing something
*P.E. **apparatus***

appeal to ask for something
that you need
*He **appealed** for help.*

appear **1** to come and be
seen
2 to seem

appearance **1** what
someone looks like
2 coming so that you can be
seen

appendix the small tube
inside the body that
sometimes causes an illness
called **appendicitis**

appetite the wish for food

applaud to clap to show that
you are pleased

applause clapping

apple a round, crisp, juicy fruit

appoint to choose someone
for a job

appointment a time when
you have arranged to go and
see someone
*an **appointment** with the
dentist*

approach to come near to

approximate nearly correct

apricot a round, soft, juicy
fruit. It has a large stone in
it and a thin, orange skin.

apron something worn over
the front of the body to
keep the clothes underneath
clean

aquarium a large, glass
container where fish are kept

arc part of the curved line of a
circle (see page 249)

arch a curved part that helps to support a bridge or building

archery shooting at a target with a bow and arrow

architect (*say* arkitect) someone whose job is to draw plans for buildings

Arctic the very cold sea and land in the north of the world

area 1 an amount of surface
2 a part of a country or place
a no smoking **area**

argue to talk about something with people who do not agree with you

argument talking in an angry or excited way to someone who does not agree with you

arithmetic finding out about numbers

ark the large boat that saved Noah, his family, and many animals from the Flood

arm the part of the body between the shoulder and the hand

armchair a comfortable chair with parts at the side for you to rest your arms on

armour 1 metal clothes worn in battles long ago
2 sheets of metal put round ships and tanks to protect them in war

armpit the part underneath the top of the arm

arms weapons

army a large group of people trained to fight on land

around 1 all round
Around the castle was a thick forest.
2 here and there
Look **around** *for it.*

arouse to wake someone up

arrange to put in order

arrangement something that has been arranged

arrest to take someone prisoner
The policeman **arrested** *the thief.*

arrive to come to the end of a journey

arrow a pointed stick that is shot from a bow

art 1 drawing and painting
2 the ability to do something
difficult

article a particular thing

artificial not natural because
it has been made by people
or machines
artificial flowers

artist someone who draws or
paints pictures

ascend (*say* a-send)
to go up

ash 1 the grey powder left
when something has been
burned
2 a kind of tree

ashamed feeling very sorry
and guilty about something

ashore on land
The sailors went *ashore*.

aside to one side
Stand *aside*!

ask to speak in order to find
out or get something

asleep sleeping

aspirin a white tablet. You
can swallow it when you
have a cold or a pain to
make you feel better.

ass a donkey

assembly the time when the
whole school meets together

assist to help

assistance help

assistant 1 someone whose
job is to help someone more
important
2 someone who serves in a
shop

assorted with different sorts
put together

astonish to surprise greatly

astonishment great surprise

astronaut someone who
travels in space

astronomer someone who
studies the stars and planets

astronomy finding out about
the stars and planets

ate see **eat**

athlete someone who trains
to be good at running,
jumping, or throwing

atlas a book of maps

atmosphere the air around
the earth

atom one of the very tiny
things that everything is
made up of

attach to join or fasten

attack to start fighting in order
to beat or hurt someone

attempt to try

attend 1 to be in a place in order to take part in something **2** to listen carefully

attendance being at a place in order to take part in something
*school **attendance***

attention 1 careful listening, reading, or thinking **2 pay attention** take notice

attic a room or rooms inside the roof of a house

attract 1 to interest **2** to make something come nearer

attractive very pleasant to look at

auction (*say* orction *or* oction) a sale when things are sold to the people who offer the most money for them

audience people who have come to a place to see or hear something

aunt your uncle's wife or the sister of one of your parents

author someone who writes books or stories

authority the power to make other people do as you say

autograph your name written by yourself

automatic able to work on its own and control itself. Slot machines are automatic.

autumn the part of the year when leaves fall off the trees and it gets colder

available ready for you to use or get

avalanche a large amount of snow, rock, or ice sliding suddenly down a mountain

avenue a road, often with trees along each side

average ordinary or usual ***average** marks of **average** height for his age*

avoid to keep out of the way of someone or something

await to wait for

awake not sleeping

award a prize that you have worked for

aware knowing about something

away 1 not here *She was **away** yesterday.* **2** to another place *He ran **away**.*

awful very bad

awkward 1 clumsy *an **awkward** child*

2 difficult to deal with
*an **awkward** customer*
3 not convenient
*an **awkward** time*

axe a tool for chopping

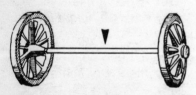

axle a rod that goes through the centre of wheels to join them to something

Bb

baby a very young child

bachelor a man who has not married

back **1** the side opposite the front

2 the part of the body between the neck and the bottom or tail

backward, backwards
  1 towards the back
  2 in the opposite way to usual

bacon dried or salty meat from a pig's back or sides

badge something worn pinned or stitched to clothes. It shows which group someone belongs to or how important he is.
*a school **badge**, a sheriff's **badge***

badger a grey animal that digs holes in the ground. It has a white face with black stripes on it.

baggage luggage

16

bail **1** one of the two pieces of wood put on the top of the stumps in cricket
2 to throw water out of a boat, using buckets
(see **stump** and **wicket**)

bait food put on a hook or in a trap to catch animals

bake to cook inside an oven

baker someone whose job is to make or sell bread and cakes

balance **1** a pair of scales for weighing things
2 to keep or make something steady
*The seal is **balancing** a ball on the end of its nose.*

balcony **1** a platform with a rail round it outside an upstairs window
2 the seats upstairs in a cinema or theatre

bald without any hair on the head

bale **1** a large bundle or package
*a **bale** of cloth*
2 ***to bale out*** to jump out of an aeroplane with a parachute

ball **1** a round object used in games
2 a big party with a lot of dancing

ballerina a woman who is a ballet-dancer

ballet a story told on the stage in dancing, mime, and music

balloon **1** a small, coloured, rubber bag that you can blow up and burst
2 a bag filled with hot air or gas so that it floats in the sky

bamboo a tall plant with stiff, hollow stems. It grows in very hot countries and is used for making furniture.

ban to say that someone must never do a certain thing

banana a long fruit with a thick yellow skin

band **1** a group of people
*a **band** of robbers*
2 some people playing musical instruments together
3 a strip of material. Bands are put round things to decorate them or to keep them together.
*a rubber **band***

bandage a strip of material for wrapping round part of the body that has been hurt

bandit an outlaw who is a robber

bang **1** the sudden, loud, hard sound an explosion makes

17

2 to hit or shut with a loud noise
Don't **bang** the door!

bangle a ring worn round the arm

banish to send someone away from a place as a punishment

banisters the posts and rail at the side of a staircase

banjo a musical instrument with strings that you play with your fingers. It is smaller and rounder than a guitar.

bank **1** a place that looks after money and valuable things for people
2 the ground near the edge of a river, canal, or lake
3 a large amount of sand or earth piled up

banner a kind of flag

banquet (*say* <u>bank</u>-wit) a big feast given by someone important

bar **1** a long piece of wood or metal
2 a block of chocolate, toffee, or soap
3 a place that serves food and drinks at a counter
*a coffee **bar***

barbed wire wire with sharp spikes in it, used for making fences

barber a man whose job is to cut men's and boys' hair

bare without any clothes or covering

bargain **1** a promise to give something in return for something else
2 something that costs much less than usual

barge a long boat with a flat

bottom. Barges are used on canals.

bark 1 to make the hard, loud sound a dog makes 2 the hard covering round a tree's trunk and branches

barley a plant grown by farmers. Its seed is used for making food and beer.

barn a large building on a farm, where things are stored

barracks an army building where soldiers live together

barrel 1 a round, wooden container with flat ends
a **barrel** of beer
2 the part like a tube at the front of a gun

barren 1 without plants
barren land
2 without fruit
a **barren** tree

barrier a fence or something that stands in the way

barrow a small cart that is pushed

base the bottom part of something

basement the rooms in a building that are below the ground

bash to hit very hard

bashful shy

basin a bowl

basket a bag made of straw or cane

bat 1 an animal like a mouse with wings
2 a piece of wood for hitting a ball in a game
3 to have a turn at playing with a bat in a game like cricket

batch a number of things together
a **batch** of letters

bath 1 a large container filled with water. You sit in it and wash yourself all over.
2 to put a baby or animal in water and wash it

bathe 1 to play or swim in the sea or a river
2 to wash part of yourself carefully and gently

bathroom the room where you can have a bath or wash

batsman the person who uses the bat in cricket or rounders

batter 1 a liquid made from flour, egg, and milk. It is used for making pancakes and frying fish.
2 to damage something by hitting it often

*The wind **battered** down the fence.*

battery a closed container with electricity inside it. You put batteries inside things like torches and radios to make them work.

battle fighting between groups of people

bawl to shout or cry loudly

bay a place where the coast bends inwards and sea fills the space

bayonet a sharp blade that can be fixed to a gun

bazaar a group of stalls selling different things to get money for something
*a church **bazaar***

beach land by the edge of the sea. It is usually covered with sand or small stones.

beacon a light or fire that warns of danger

bead a small, round object with a hole through the middle. Beads are threaded on string to make necklaces and bracelets.

beak the hard part round a bird's mouth

beaker a kind of tall cup. Some beakers have no handle.

beam **1** a long piece of wood
2 a line of light
3 to smile very happily

bean a vegetable. Beans are round seeds and some sorts grow inside long green pods that can also be eaten.
*French **beans**, broad **beans***

beanbag a small cloth bag filled with dried beans, used in games

bear **1** to carry
*The donkey **bore** the load patiently.*
2 to put up with
*He could not have **borne** any more pain.*
3 to give birth to
*Their baby was **born** yesterday.*
4 a large animal with very thick fur

beard hair growing on a man's chin

beast **1** any big animal

2 a horrible person
*Beauty and the **Beast***

beat **1** to do better than someone else
*You **beat** me last time.*
2 to hit often
*The horse had been **beaten** with a stick.*
3 to stir very hard

beautiful **1** very attractive
*a **beautiful** face*
2 very pleasant
*a **beautiful** day*

beauty something or someone beautiful

became see **become**

because for the reason that
*I got wet **because** it rained.*

beckon to move your hand to show someone that you want him to come nearer

become to come to be
*It suddenly **became** very cold yesterday.*

bedroom the room where you sleep

bee an insect that can fly, sting, and make honey

beech a kind of tree

beef meat from an ox, bull, or cow

beehive a kind of box for keeping bees in

beehive

beer a strong brown drink

beetle an insect that flies with one pair of wings and uses the other pair as wing cases

beetroot a round, dark red vegetable

before **1** earlier than
*I was here **before** you.*
2 in front of
*It vanished **before** my eyes.*

began see **begin**

beggar someone who lives by asking other people for money, clothes, or food

begin to start
*I'm **beginning** to understand.*
*He **began** school last week.*
*I have **begun** to learn the piano.*

beginner someone who has just started learning something

beginning the start of something

begun see **begin**

behave 1 to show good or bad manners in front of other people
*He's **behaved** badly, she's **behaving** well.*
2 ***Behave yourself**!* Be good!

behaviour how you behave

behind at the back of
*He hid **behind** the wall.*

belief what someone believes

believe to feel sure that something is true

bell a hollow piece of metal that rings when it is hit

bellow to shout and make a lot of noise like an angry bull

belly the stomach

belong 1 to be someone's
*That pen **belongs** to me.*
2 to be part of something
3 to be in the proper place

below underneath
*Write your address **below** your name.*

belt a stiff band worn round the waist

bench a wooden or stone seat for more than one person

bend 1 to make something curved or not straight
2 to lean over so that your head is nearer to the ground
*He **bent** down and looked at his shoes.*

beneath underneath

bent see **bend**

beret (*say* berray)
a round, soft, flat hat

berry any small, round fruit with seeds in it. Some berries are poisonous.

beside at the side of
*a house **beside** the sea*

besides as well as
*ten people **besides** me*

best better than any other
*my **best** friend*

betray 1 to give away a secret
2 to give information about your friends or country to the enemy

better 1 less bad
***better** than me at swimming*
2 well again
*I'm **better** now, thank you.*

between 1 in the middle of two people or things
*I sat **between** Mum and Dad.*
2 among

*Share the money **between** you.*

beware be careful

bewildered very puzzled

bewitched under a spell

beyond further than
*Don't go **beyond** the end of the road.*

Bible the holy book that is read in all Christian churches

bicycle, bike a machine with two wheels and pedals, that you can ride

bill   1 a piece of paper that tells you how much money you owe
2 a bird's beak

billiards a game played on a long table with rods used to hit three small balls

billy-goat a male goat

bind to tie together
*The prisoner's hands were **bound** behind his back.*

bingo a game where each person has a card with different numbers on it. He marks the numbers off when they are called.

binoculars a special pair of glasses like two tubes joined together. When you look through them, things far away seem much nearer.

birch a kind of tree

bird any animal with feathers, wings, and a beak

birth the beginning of life, when a baby leaves its mother and starts to breathe

birthday the date each year when you remember the day someone was born

biscuit a kind of small, thin, dry cake

bishop a priest who is in charge of other priests

bit   1 a very small amount of something
2 the part of a bridle that goes into a horse's mouth
3 see **bite**

bitch a female dog

bite to use the teeth to cut into something
*Your dog's **bitten** me.*
*Stop **biting** your nails!*
*She **bit** into the cream cake.*

bitter not sweet

blackberry a small, soft, black berry that grows on bushes

blackbird a bird often seen in gardens. The male is black with an orange beak, but the female is brown.

blackboard a piece of black or dark green wood that you can write on with chalk

blacksmith someone whose job is to make horseshoes and other things out of iron

blade 1 the flat, sharp part of a knife or sword
2 something shaped like a blade
a **blade** of grass

blame to say that it is because of a certain person or thing that something bad has happened

blancmange (say bla-monj) a kind of jelly made from sugar, milk, and flour

blank with nothing written or drawn on it
a **blank** page

blanket a thick cover used on a bed

blast 1 sudden, rushing wind or air
2 to blow up

blaze to burn brightly

blazer a kind of jacket. A blazer usually has a badge on its top pocket.

bleach to make something white

bleak cold, miserable, and windy
a **bleak** day

bleat to make the sound sheep make

bleed to lose blood
His nose **bled** for ten minutes.

blend to mix together

bless to ask God to look after someone and make him happy
God **bless** you.

blew see **blow**

blind 1 not able to see
2 a screen that you pull down to cover a window

blink to close your eyes and open them again very quickly

blister a small swelling on the skin. It has liquid inside and hurts when you touch it.

blizzard a storm with a lot of snow and wind

block 1 a thick piece of something solid like wood or stone
2 to be in the way so that something cannot get through

blond, blonde with fair hair

blood a red liquid that moves round inside the body

bloom **1** to be in flower
*Roses **bloom** in summer.*
2 to be very healthy

blossom flowers on a tree

blot a spot of ink spilt on something

blotting-paper thick paper that dries ink quickly

blouse a piece of clothing worn on the top half of the body by women and girls
*a **blouse** and skirt*

blow **1** to make air come out of the mouth
*She **blew** the candles out and cut the cake.*
2 to move along with the wind
*Tiles were **blown** off the roof.*

bluebell a wild plant with flowers like tiny blue bells

blunder **1** to make a big mistake
2 to move about very clumsily

blunt not sharp
*a **blunt** knife*

blur to make something look not clear. Smudged writing is blurred.

blush to go red in the face because you feel shy or guilty

boar a wild pig

board **1** a long piece of thin wood
2 stiff cardboard
3 to get on an aeroplane, bus, ship, or train

boast to talk in a way that shows you are much too proud of yourself and what you can do

boat something that floats and has room in it for taking people or things over water

body **1** all of a person or animal that can be seen or touched
*a dead **body***
2 all of a person except his legs, arms, and head

bodyguard a person or persons whose job is to protect someone

bog a piece of ground so wet and soft that your feet sink into it

boil **1** to heat liquid until it bubbles

2 to cook something in hot, bubbling water
3 a big painful spot on the skin

boiler a large container in which water is heated

bold brave and not afraid

bolt **1** to rush off
2 to swallow food quickly without chewing it
3 a kind of sliding fastener used on doors
4 a thick metal pin like a screw

bomb a weapon that blows up and does a lot of damage

bone any of the separate parts of a skeleton

bonfire a large fire built in the open air

bonnet **1** a hat that is tied under the chin
2 the part of a car that covers the engine

book **1** sheets of paper fastened together and fixed to a cover
2 to arrange for a seat to be kept for you. You can book seats on coaches and trains and at theatres and cinemas.

bookcase a piece of furniture made for holding books

boom to make a loud, deep sound
*The guns **boomed** away in the distance.*

boomerang a curved stick that comes back to the person who throws it

boot **1** a kind of shoe that also covers the ankle
2 the part of a car for carrying luggage

border **1** the narrow part along the edge of something
*a **border** of flowers*
2 the line where two countries meet

bore **1** to make someone tired by being dull
*a **boring** film*
2 to make a hole with a tool
3 see **bear**

born, borne see **bear**

borrow to get the use of something for a short time and agree to give it back

boss the person who is in charge

both the two of them
*He took **both** of the cakes.*

bother **1** to worry or annoy someone
2 to take trouble over doing something

bottle a glass container for liquids that is narrow at the top
*a milk **bottle***

bottom **1** the lowest part of anything
2 the part of the body that you sit on

bough a large branch

bought see **buy**

boulder a large, smooth rock

bounce to spring back after hitting something hard

bound **1** to leap
2 see **bind**

boundary a line marking the edge of some land

bouquet (*say* boo-kay)
a bunch of flowers

bow[1] (*rhymes with* go)
1 a strip of bent wood with string joined to each end. It is used for shooting arrows.
2 a wooden rod with strong hairs stretched along it and joined to each end, for playing the violin
3 a knot with loops

bow[2] (*rhymes with* cow)
to bend forwards to show respect
*He **bowed** to the Queen.*

bowl (*say* bole)
1 a round, open container for liquid or food
2 to send a ball to the batsman

box **1** a container with a lid
*a cardboard **box***
2 to fight with the fists

boy a male child or teenager

brace a piece of wire worn across teeth to straighten them

bracelet beads, a chain, or a ring worn round the arm

braces a pair of straps worn to keep up trousers

bracket **1** a piece of metal fixed to a wall to support something
2 one of a pair of marks like these ( )

brag to talk in a way that shows you are much too proud of yourself and what you can do

brain the part inside the top of the head that controls the body. It also makes people able to think and remember.

brake the part of a car or bicycle that makes it slow down or stop

bramble a blackberry bush or a prickly bush like it

branch a part that sticks out from the trunk of a tree

brand **1** a mark to show the maker or owner
2 a certain kind of goods
*a new **brand** of tea*

brass a yellow metal made by mixing copper with another metal called zinc

brave **1** ready and able to bear pain or danger
2 a male American Indian

bravery the ability to do brave deeds

bray to make the harsh sound a donkey makes

bread a food made by baking dough in loaves

breadth the measurement or distance across something

break **1** to snap, smash, or crack
*The cup **broke** when I dropped it.*
2 to fail to keep a law or promise

*He's **broken** the rules.*
3 a short rest from work

breakfast the first meal of the day

breath the air that a person breathes

breathe to take air into your lungs through your nose or mouth and send it out again

breed to keep animals in order to get young ones from them
*Last year he **bred** rabbits.*

breeze a gentle wind

brick a small, oblong block used in building

bride a woman on the day she gets married

bridegroom a man on the day he gets married

bridesmaid a girl or woman who walks behind the bride at her wedding

bridge something built to go over a river, railway, or road

bridle the parts of a harness used for controlling a horse (see **harness**)

brief short
*a **brief** talk*

brigade an organized group of people in uniform

bright **1** shining
*a **bright** star*
2 intelligent
*a **bright** boy*
3 cheerful
*a **bright** smile*

brilliant very bright
***brilliant** light*
*a **brilliant** scientist*

brim **1** the edge round the top of a container
*a cup filled to the **brim***
2 the part of a hat that sticks out round the edge

bring **1** to carry here
***Bring** your book.*
2 to lead here
*Yesterday he **brought** his friend.*

brink the edge of a dangerous place

brisk quick and lively

bristle a short, stiff hair like the hairs on a brush

brittle likely to break or snap

broad measuring a lot from side to side
*a **broad** river*

broadcast a television or radio programme

broke, broken see **break**

bronze a brown metal made by mixing copper and tin

brooch (*rhymes with* coach) a piece of jewellery worn pinned to clothing

brook a small stream

broom a stiff brush for sweeping, with a long handle

broth a thin soup made from meat and vegetables

brother a man or boy who has the same parents as another person

brought see **bring**

brow **1** the forehead
2 the top of a hill

Brownie a junior Guide

bruise a coloured mark that comes on the skin when it has been hit hard

brush a tool with short, stiff hairs. Brushes are used for making hair tidy, cleaning, sweeping, scrubbing, and painting.

bubble **1** a small ball of air inside liquid
2 to be full of bubbles

buck **1** a male deer, hare, or rabbit
2 to leap like a horse about to throw someone off its back

bucket a container with a handle but no lid, used for carrying liquid

buckle a kind of fastening used on belts or straps

bud a flower or leaf before it has opened

budge to move slightly
I've pushed hard but it won't budge.

budgerigar a small, brightly coloured bird kept as a pet

buffalo a kind of wild ox. Buffaloes are found in Africa, India, and North America.

buffet (*say* buffay) a place where you can get drinks and snacks

bugle a small brass musical instrument that you blow

build to make something by putting things carefully on top of one another
*Last autumn we **built** a huge bonfire.*

building something that has been built. Houses, schools, theatres, shops, and churches are all buildings.

built see **build**

bulb 1 a glass electric lamp shaped like a pear
2 something that looks like an onion and is planted in soil. Daffodils, tulips, and some other flowers grow from bulbs.

bulge to swell out

bulk a large amount

bull a male ox, elephant, or whale

bulldozer a heavy machine for clearing land

bullet a small lump of metal made to be fired from a gun

bullock a young, male ox

bully someone who attacks or threatens a weaker person

bulrush a tall plant that grows near water

bulrushes

bump 1 to knock against something by accident
*The giant **bumped** his head on the ceiling.*
2 a swelling

bumper a bar along the front or back of a car. It protects the car if it hits something.

bunch a group of things joined or tied together
*a **bunch** of bananas*

bundle a group of things tied together

bungalow a house without any upstairs rooms

bunk a bed that has another bed above or below it

buoy (*say* boy)
something that floats on the sea, but is fixed to one spot to guide ships

burden something that has to be carried

burglar someone who gets into a building to steal things

burial (*say* berrial)
the burying of a dead person

burn 1 to hurt or damage something with fire or heat
2 to be on fire
*The house **burnt** for an hour.*

burrow a hole in the ground that an animal lives in

burst to break open suddenly because there is too much inside
*The balloon **burst** when I blew it up.*

bury to put something in a hole in the ground and cover it over

bus a kind of big car with a lot of seats, that anyone can travel in

bush a plant that looks like a small tree

business (*say* biznis)
1 a person's work
2 a shop or firm

bustle to hurry in a busy or fussy way

busy 1 doing things all the time

2 full of activity
*a **busy** street*

butcher someone who cuts up meat and sells it

butter a yellow food made from cream. It is spread on bread and biscuits.

buttercup a wild flower with shiny yellow petals

butterfly an insect with large white or coloured wings

butterscotch hard toffee made from sugar and butter

button a fastener sewn on clothes. It fits into a hole or loop.

buy to get something by giving money for it
*I **bought** this bike from him yesterday.*

buzz to make the sound a bee makes

Cc

cab 1 the part of a lorry, bus, or train where the driver sits
2 a taxi

cabbage a vegetable with a lot of green leaves

cabin 1 a room in a ship or aeroplane
2 a small hut
*a log **cabin***

cabinet a kind of cupboard with drawers

cable strong, thick wire or rope

cackle to laugh and make the sound a hen makes

cactus a plant with a thick green stem and thick green branches, covered in prickles. Cacti grow in hot, dry places and do not need much water.

café (*say* kaffay)
a place where you can buy a drink, a snack, or a meal

cafeteria a kind of café where you fetch your own food from the counter

cage a large box with bars

across it for keeping animals in

cake a food made with flour, butter, eggs, and sugar
*fruit **cake**, chocolate **cake***

calamity something very bad that happens suddenly

calculator a machine that can do sums

calendar a list showing all the days, weeks, and months in a year

calf　**1** the back part of the leg between the knee and the ankle
2 a young ox, elephant, or whale
*two **calves***

caliper a pair of metal bars worn to support a weak leg

call　**1** to speak loudly
2 to give a name to someone or something
3 to tell someone to come to you

calm　**1** still
*a **calm** sea*
2 not noisy or excited

calves more than one **calf**

came see **come**

camel a big animal with one or two humps on its back. Camels are used instead of horses in deserts, because they can travel for a long time without eating or drinking.

camera a kind of box that you put a film in and use for taking photographs

camouflage (*say* cam-er-flarj)
to hide something by making it look like other things that are near it. Most wild animals are camouflaged by their colour or shape, when they are not moving.

camp　**1** a group of tents or huts where people live for a short time
2 *to go camping* to have a holiday living in a tent

can　**1** to be able to
*I **can't** swim.*
*He **could** read before he started school. I **couldn't**.*
2 a tin

canal a kind of river made by people, so that boats can go

33

straight from one place to another

canary a small yellow bird that sings

candle a stick of wax with string through the centre. It gives light as it burns.

candlestick something that holds a candle firm

cane **1** the hard stem of some plants
2 a long, thin stick

cannon a big gun that fired heavy metal balls

canoe (*say* ca-<u>noo</u>) a light, narrow boat that you move by using a paddle

canter one of the ways a horse can move. It is faster than a trot but slower than a gallop.

canvas strong material for making things like tents

capable able to do something *You're **capable** of better work.*

capacity the largest amount a container can hold

cape a short cloak

capital **1** the most important city in a country *London is the **capital** of England.*

2 one of the big letters put at the beginning of names and sentences. A, B, C, D, and so on are **capital letters.**

capsule **1** something that looks like a sweet, but has medicine inside. It has to be swallowed whole.
2 a separate part at the front of a space ship. It can move on its own away from the main part.

captain **1** an officer in the army or navy
2 someone who is in charge of a team

captive a person or animal that has been captured

capture **1** to take prisoner
2 to get something by fighting for it

caramel soft toffee

caravan a home that looks like a van or a cart with a cover over it. It can be pulled from place to place.

carburettor the part of an engine that mixes the petrol with air

card **1** thick, stiff paper
2 a piece of card with a picture and a message on it. You send cards to people at special times like Christmas.
3 one of a set of small

pieces of card with numbers or pictures on them, used in games

cardboard very thick, strong paper
*a **cardboard** box*

cardigan a kind of knitted jacket

care **1** worry or trouble
2 *to take care of* to look after
3 *to care for* to look after
4 *to care about* to be very interested in something

careful making sure that you do things safely and well
*a **careful** driver*

careless not careful

caretaker someone whose job is to look after a building

cargo things taken by ship or aeroplane from one place to another
***cargoes** of fruit*

carnation a garden plant with white, pink, or red flowers that smell very sweet

carnival a gay procession with people wearing fancy dress

carol a happy song sung at Christmas

carpenter someone whose

job is to make things out of wood

carpet a thick cover for the floor

carriage **1** one of the separate parts of a train where the people sit
2 a kind of box on wheels pulled by horses, that people can travel in

carrot an orange vegetable shaped like a cone

carry to take people, animals, or things from one place to another

cart a kind of box on wheels. It is pulled by a horse or pushed by a person.

carton a light container made of cardboard or plastic

cartoon **1** a film that uses drawings instead of actors
*a Mickey Mouse **cartoon***
2 a drawing that tells a joke

cartridge **1** a small container with a bullet and an explosive inside
2 a small tube filled with ink. It fits inside a pen so that you do not need to fill the pen with ink from a bottle.
*a **cartridge** pen*

carve **1** to cut something hard into a shape

2 to cut off slices of meat

case **1** a container
a pencil case
2 a suitcase

cash coins or paper money

casket a small box for keeping precious things in

cassette a small closed container with a reel of tape inside it for making sounds. You put it inside a tape-recorder and it can be used straight away.

cast **1** a shape made by pouring liquid metal or plaster into a mould
2 all the actors in a play
3 to throw
*He **cast** his net into the sea to catch fish.*

castaway someone who has been shipwrecked

castle a large, strong house with very thick, stone walls. Castles were built long ago to keep the people inside them safe from their enemies.
*Windsor **Castle***

catalogue a list

catapult a piece of elastic joined to a stick shaped like a Y for shooting small stones

catch **1** to capture
2 to get hold of something

3 to get an illness
*I **caught** a cold last week.*

caterpillar a long, creeping creature that will turn into a butterfly or moth

cathedral a big, important church
*Durham **Cathedral***

catkin one of the tiny flowers that hang down in clusters on some trees

cattle cows and bulls kept by a farmer

caught see **catch**

cauldron

cauldron a large pot used for cooking
*a witch's **cauldron***

cauliflower a vegetable with a thick white stalk covered in small, hard, white flowers

cause to make something happen

cautious only doing what is safe
*a **cautious** man*

cavalry a group of men trained to fight while riding horses

cave a big hole under the ground or inside a mountain

cavern a large cave

cease to stop doing something

ceiling the flat part that covers the top of a room

celebrate to do special things to show you are very happy about something. Every year people celebrate Christmas.

celebration a party for something special

celery a vegetable with white stalks that can be eaten raw

cell one of the small rooms where prisoners are kept in a prison

cellar a room underneath a building. Cellars are used for storing things.

cement a mixture of clay and lime used in building to stick things together

cemetery (*say* sem-er-tree) a place where dead people are buried

centigrade a way of measuring temperature that gives 0 degrees for freezing water and 100 degrees for boiling water.

centimetre a measure for length
*My ruler is 30 **centimetres** long.*

centipede a long, creeping creature with a lot of tiny legs

centre the point or part in the middle

century a hundred years

cereal **1** any plant grown by farmers for its seed
2 a food made from the seed of cereal plants and eaten at breakfast with milk

ceremony (*say* serimony) something important and serious that is done in front of other people
*a marriage **ceremony***

certain **1** sure
*Are you **certain**?*
2 one in particular
*a **certain** person*

certificate a piece of paper that says you have done something special

chaffinch a small bird. Its front is red and it has white marks on its wings.

chain a line made of metal rings fastened together

chair a seat for one person

chalet (*say* shallay)
a small, wooden house with a large roof

chalk **1** a kind of soft white rock
2 a soft white stick used for writing on blackboards

challenge to ask someone to try to do better than you at something

champion **1** someone who is the best in his sport
2 an animal or plant that wins a competition

championship a competition to decide on the champion

chance **1** a time when you can do something that you cannot do at other times
*This is your last **chance**.*
2 the way things happen that have not been planned
*I saw him by **chance** on the bus.*

change **1** to make or become different
2 to give something and get something in return
3 the money that you get back when you give more money than is needed to pay for something

channel **1** a narrow sea
*the English **Channel***
2 a narrow way in the ground that water moves along

chapel a kind of church

chapter a part of a book

character **1** someone in a story
2 the sort of person you are

charcoal a black stick used for drawing

charge **1** to ask a certain price
2 to rush at something to attack it
3 *in charge* with the job of telling other people what they should do or how they should do it

chariot a kind of cart with two wheels, pulled by horses. Chariots were used long ago for fighting and racing.

chariot

charity gifts of money or help to people who need it

charm **1** a magic spell
2 a small ornament worn to bring good luck
3 to cast a spell over someone or something

chart **1** a big map
2 a large sheet of paper with information on it

chase to run after and try to catch a person or animal

chat to talk in a friendly way about things that are not important

chatter **1** to talk a lot or very quickly
2 to make a rattling noise
*His teeth **chattered** with fear.*

chauffeur (*say* show-fur) someone whose job is to drive another person's car for him

cheap costing less than usual

cheat **1** to make another person believe what is not true so that you can get something from him
2 to try to do well in a test or game, by breaking the rules

check **1** a pattern of squares
2 to go over something to make sure it is correct

cheek **1** the side of the face below the eye
2 rude behaviour or speech

cheer to shout to show you are pleased or that you want your team to win

cheerful looking or sounding happy
*a **cheerful** face*

cheese solid food with a strong flavour, made from milk

chemist someone whose job is to make or sell medicines

cherry a small, round, red or black fruit with a stone in it

chest **1** a big, strong box
2 the front part of the body between the neck and the waist

chestnut **1** a kind of tree
2 the shiny brown nut that grows on a chestnut tree

chew **1** to keep biting food while you eat it
2 a kind of sweet

chicken a young bird kept for its meat and eggs

chicken-pox an illness that gives you red spots that itch

chief 1 the most important **2** the person in charge

child 1 a young boy or girl **2** a son or daughter
*two **children***

chill 1 a bad cold that makes you feel hot and dizzy **2** to make something cold

chime to make a tune like church bells

chimney a tall pipe inside the wall of a house. Smoke from the fire moves up the chimney so that it can get out through the roof.

chimpanzee an African animal like a large monkey with long arms and no tail

chin the part of the face that is under the mouth

china cups, saucers, and plates made of very thin, delicate pottery

chip 1 a small piece of potato that is fried **2** to break or knock small pieces off something
*a **chipped** vase*

chisel a tool with a short,

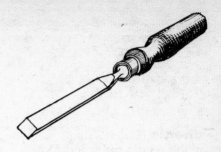

sharp edge, for cutting stone or wood

chocolate sweet food made from cocoa and sugar

choice 1 choosing **2** what you have chosen

choir (*say* kwire) a group of people who sing together

choke 1 to find it hard to get your breath because of something in your throat
*The smoke made him **choke**.*
2 to block up something
*The pond was **choked** with weeds.*

choose to take one thing instead of another, because you want to
*Which car have you **chosen**? Last time you **chose** to go to the zoo.*

chop 1 to cut something by hitting it hard with a sharp tool

2 a small, thick slice of pork, lamb, or mutton

chopsticks a pair of thin sticks that Chinese and Japanese people use instead of a knife and fork

chorus (*say* kor-uss) the words repeated after every verse in a poem or song

chose, chosen see **choose**

christen to give a baby its Christian name in church and welcome it into God's family
The minister **christened** *the baby yesterday.*

Christian someone who believes in Jesus Christ

Christmas the 25th December that is kept as Jesus Christ's birthday

chrome, chromium (*say* krome, krome-ium) a bright, shiny metal that looks like silver

chrysalis (*say* kriss-a-liss) the cover a caterpillar makes round itself before it changes into a butterfly or moth

chrysanthemum an autumn flower with a lot of petals that grows in gardens

chuckle to laugh to yourself

chunk a thick lump
a **chunk** of meat

church a building where people worship God

churn **1** a large container for milk
2 a machine for turning milk into butter

cigar a roll of tobacco leaves for smoking

cigarette a thin tube of paper with tobacco inside it for smoking

cinders the grey pieces left when coal has finished burning

cinema a place where people go to see films

circle **1** the shape of a coin or wheel. The edge of a circle is always the same distance from the centre. (See the list of shapes on page 248)
2 the curved line round the edge of a circle

circular like a circle

circus a show held in a big tent or building with animals, acrobats, and clowns

city a big town

clad dressed

claim to ask for something that belongs to you

41

clang to make the loud, ringing sound a heavy metal door makes when you shut it

clank to make the hard sound that heavy metal chains make when they bang against each other

clap to make a noise by hitting the palm of one hand with the palm of the other

clash 1 to make the sound cymbals make
2 to disagree with someone

clasp to hold tightly

class a group of pupils who learn things together

clatter to make the rattling sound a horse's hooves make on the road

claw one of the hard, sharp nails that some animals have on their feet

clay a sticky kind of earth used for making things, because it keeps its shape and goes hard

clean 1 not dirty
a **clean** face
2 to make something clean

clear 1 easy to understand, see, or hear
a **clear** photograph, a **clear** voice
2 free from things you do not want
a **clear** road, a **clear** day
3 to make something clear
Please **clear** the table.

clench to close your teeth, fingers, or fist tightly to show that you are determined to do something

clerk (*rhymes with* park) someone who sorts out papers and writes letters in an office

clever able to learn and understand things easily

click the short, sharp sound an electric light switch makes

cliff a steep rock close to the sea

climate the sort of weather that a place usually gets at different times of the year

climb to go up or down something high

cling to hold tightly on to someone or something
The child was afraid and **clung** to its mother.

clinic a kind of hospital

clip 1 to cut something with scissors or a tool like scissors
He **clipped** the hedge.

2 a fastener for keeping things together or in place
*a paper **clip***

cloak a very loose coat without sleeves

cloakroom the room where you hang your coat

clock a machine that shows you what time it is

clockwise in the direction a clock's hands move in

clockwork able to work when it is wound up like a clock. Clockwork toys can move by themselves.

clog a kind of shoe with a wooden sole

close¹ (*rhymes with* dose)
1 very near
***close** to the fire*
2 careful
*a **close** look*
3 a street closed at one end

close² (*rhymes with* doze)
1 to shut
*The shops are **closing** early today.*
2 to end

cloth 1 material for making things like clothes and curtains
2 a piece of cloth for cleaning or covering something

clothes, clothing things worn to cover the body

cloud 1 something white, grey, or black that floats in the sky. Clouds are made of drops of water that often fall as rain.
2 dust or smoke that looks like a cloud

clout to hit hard with your hand

clover a wild flower. Each of its leaves is like three small leaves joined together.

clown someone in a circus who wears funny clothes and make-up and makes people laugh

club 1 a group of people who meet together because they are interested in the same thing
2 a thick stick used as a weapon
3 a black clover leaf printed on some playing cards

clue something that helps you to find the answer to a puzzle

clump a group of trees or plants growing close together

clumsy likely to knock things over or drop things, because you move badly

clung see **cling**

cluster **1** a group of things growing together
2 a group of people, animals, or things gathered round something

clutch **1** to snatch at something
2 to hold tightly

coach **1** a bus that takes people on long journeys
2 one of the separate parts of a train, where people sit
3 a kind of box on wheels pulled by several horses, that people can travel in

coal hard, black stuff that is burned to make heat

coarse not delicate or smooth. Sacks are made of coarse material.

coast the edge of land next to the sea

coat something with long sleeves that people wear outside over other clothes

cobbler someone whose job is to mend shoes

cobweb a thin, sticky net spun by a spider to trap insects

cock a male bird

cockerel a young, male bird kept with hens

cocoa a brown powder used to make a hot drink that tastes of chocolate

coconut a big, round, hard seed that grows on palm trees. It has a sweet white food and liquid inside.

cod a large sea fish that can be eaten

code **1** a set of signs or letters for sending messages secretly or quickly
2 a set of rules
*the Highway **Code***

coffee a hot drink. It is made from cooked seeds crushed into a brown powder.

coffin the long box in which a dead person is put

coil to wind rope or wire into rings

coin a piece of metal money

coke **1** black stuff that is made from coal and can be burnt instead of coal
2 a brown, fizzy drink

cold **1** like ice or snow feels

2 an illness that makes you sneeze and blow your nose a lot

collage (*say* col-arj) a picture made from small pieces of paper and material

collapse 1 to fall to pieces **2** to fall down because you are ill

collar 1 the part that goes round the neck of clothes such as shirts and jackets **2** a band put round the neck of a dog or cat

collect 1 to bring things together from different places *I **collect** foreign coins.* **2** to go and get someone or something

collection a set of things that have been collected *a stamp **collection***

collector someone who collects things as a hobby or as a job

college 1 a kind of school **2** a place where people can carry on learning about something when they are too old for school

collide to hit someone or something by accident while you are moving

collie a black and white sheep dog

colliery a coal mine

collision a crash between two moving things

colour 1 red, blue, and green are colours (see the list of colours on page 254) **2** to use paint or crayon on something

colt a young, male horse

column 1 a list of numbers or short lines of words, each below the one that comes before it **2** a thick stone post that supports something or decorates a building *Nelson's **Column***

comb 1 a strip of plastic, wood, or metal with a row of thin parts like teeth, for making hair tidy **2** to search a place very carefully

combine to join or mix together

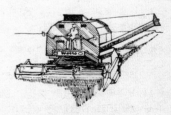

combine-harvester a machine that cuts down corn and gets the seed out of it

45

come **1** to move here
I **came** as soon as I could.
2 to arrive
Has the letter **come** yet?
It's **coming** soon.

comedian someone who entertains people by making them laugh

comedy a funny play

comfortable **1** pleasant to be in, to sit on, or to wear
a **comfortable** chair
2 free from pain or worry

comic **1** funny
2 a paper with stories told in pictures

comma a mark like this , to divide parts of a sentence

command **1** to tell someone to do something
2 to be in charge of something

common **1** usual
a **common** illness
2 a piece of land that anyone can use
Wimbledon **Common**

commotion a lot of noise

communication
1 a message
2 a way of sending or getting a message

community the people living in one place

companion a friend who is with you

company **1** having an animal or another person with you so that you are not lonely
The cat kept her **company**.
2 a group of people who do things together
a **company** of actors

compare to see how like each other some things are

compass an instrument that always shows where north is. A compass helps you to find your way when you are lost.

compasses an instrument for drawing circles
a pair of **compasses**

compete to take part in a race or competition

competition a kind of test or game with a prize for the person who wins

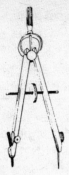

compasses

complain to say that you are not pleased about something

complete **1** whole
2 to come to the end of doing something

complicated **1** with a lot of different parts
*a **complicated** machine*
2 difficult
*a **complicated** sum*

compliment words that praise the person you are speaking to or writing to

composer someone who writes music

composition a story you have made up and written down

computer a machine that can work things out very quickly, if it is given the right instructions and information

conceal to hide

conceited too proud of yourself and what you can do

concentrate to think hard about one thing

concern **1** to be important or interesting to someone or something
2 *concerned* worried

concert an entertainment with music

concrete a mixture of cement and sand used for making buildings, paths, and bridges

condense to make something smaller. Condensed milk is thicker than ordinary milk and takes up less space.

condition the state something is in

conductor **1** someone who sells tickets on a bus and looks after the passengers
2 someone who stands facing a band, choir or orchestra and keeps everyone playing together

cone **1** the shape of a witch's hat or an ice-cream cornet (see the list of shapes on pages 248–9)
2 a wooden case for seeds that grows on some trees
*a fir **cone***

confess to say that you have done wrong

confetti tiny pieces of coloured paper that are thrown over a bride and bridegroom

confident **1** brave and not afraid
*a **confident** swimmer*
2 sure about something

confuse to mix up

congratulate to tell someone how pleased you are about something special that has happened to him

conjuror someone who entertains people by doing tricks that look like magic

conker the hard, shiny brown nut that grows on a horse-chestnut tree

connect to join together

conquer to beat in a battle or war

conscious (*say* kon-shuss) awake and able to understand what is happening around you

consider to think carefully about something

considerable large
*a **considerable** amount of money*

considerate kind and thoughtful in the way you behave towards other people

consonant any letter of the alphabet except a e i o u and sometimes y

constable an ordinary policeman or policewoman

constellation a group of stars

construct to build

contain to have something inside

container anything that you can put other things into. Buckets, cups, bags, boxes, and jars are all containers.

contented happy with what you have

contents what is inside a container or a book

contest a competition

continent one of the seven very large areas of land in the world (see the list of continents on page 252)

continue to go on doing something

contradict to say that someone is saying something that is not true

control to be in charge of

something and be able to make it do what you want

convenient easy to get at or use

convent a place where nuns live and work together

conversation talking and listening to another person

convict a criminal who is in prison

convince to make someone believe something

cook **1** to get food ready to eat by heating it
2 someone whose job is to cook

cookery cooking food

cool not warm
a **cool** drink

copper a shiny brown or red metal used for making pipes and coins

copy **1** to write down or draw what is already written down or drawn
She **copied** the poem in her best writing.
2 to do exactly the same as someone else

coral a kind of rock made in the sea from the bodies of tiny creatures. Coral can be pink, white, or black.

cord thin rope

core the part in the middle of something
an apple **core**

corgi a kind of light brown dog with very short legs and pointed ears

cork a piece of bark from a special kind of tree. It is put into the top of a bottle to close it.

corkscrew a tool for getting corks out of bottles

corn any plant grown by farmers for its seed

corner the point where two edges or streets meet

cornet **1** a wafer shaped like a cone for holding ice-cream

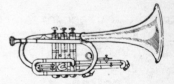

2 a musical instrument made of brass, that you blow

cornflakes a kind of food made from corn, eaten with milk at breakfast

coronation the time when someone is crowned as king or queen

corpse a dead body

correct without any mistakes

corridor a long, narrow way inside a big building or train. It has doors along it and people go down it to get from one room to another.

cosmonaut someone who travels in space

cost **1** to have a certain price
*The bike **cost** a lot more before the sales.*
2 the price something is sold at

costume **1** clothes worn on the stage
2 clothes like ones worn long ago

cosy warm and comfortable

cottage a small house in the country

cotton **1** thread for sewing
2 a light cloth made from a plant that grows in hot countries
*a cool **cotton** dress*

cotton wool soft, white, fluffy, cotton stuff. Cotton wool is used in looking after babies and injured people and in packing delicate things.

couch a settee or sofa

cough to make a sudden, loud noise to get rid of something

in your throat. Smoke and bad colds make people cough.

could see **can**

council a group of people chosen to plan and decide what should be done in a place
*a City **Council***

count **1** to say the numbers in order
2 to use numbers to find out how many people or things there are in a place

counter **1** the long table where you are served in a shop, cafeteria, or bank
2 a small, round, flat piece of plastic used for playing some games

country **1** a land with its own people and laws. England, Australia, and China are all countries.
2 the countryside

countryside land with farms and villages, away from towns

county one of the large areas Britain and Ireland are divided into

couple two
*a **couple** of sweets*

coupon a kind of ticket that

you can change for a free gift. Some coupons make you able to buy things for less money than usual.

courage the ability to be brave

course **1** the direction something takes
a ship's **course**
2 a piece of ground where some kinds of sport take place

court **1** a piece of ground marked out for a game like netball or tennis
2 the place where a king or queen is living and the people who are with them
3 the place where people decide whether someone is guilty of breaking the law

cousin the child of your aunt or uncle

cover **1** to put one thing over or round another thing
2 something used for covering things

coward someone who cannot face up to danger

cowboy a man who rides round looking after the cattle on a large farm in America

cowslip a yellow wild flower that grows in the spring

crab an animal with a shell, claws, and ten legs that lives in or near the sea

crack **1** to make the sudden, sharp noise a dry twig makes when you snap it
2 a line on the surface of something where it has been partly broken. Cracks can come in walls, ceilings, cups, and plates.

cracker **1** a paper tube with a toy and paper hat inside. It bangs when two people pull it apart.
Christmas **crackers**
2 a thin biscuit eaten with butter or cheese

crackle to make the cracking sounds burning wood makes

cradle a baby's bed

craftsman someone who is very good at doing difficult work with his hands

crafty clever at planning things so that you get your own way

crane

51

crane **1** a machine on wheels for lifting very heavy things
2 a large bird with very long legs

crash **1** the loud noise made when something heavy is dropped and smashed
2 to hit something with a loud noise
The car **crashed** in the fog.

crate a container for carrying bottles or other things that break easily

crawl **1** to move on your hands and knees
2 to move slowly

crayon **1** a stick of coloured wax used for drawing
2 a coloured pencil

crazy likely to do strange or silly things

creak to make a loud, rough, squeaking noise. New shoes, doors that need oiling, and old wooden stairs creak.

cream **1** the thick part on the top of milk
2 the colour of cream
3 something that looks like cream and is put on the skin
hand **cream**

crease to make a line in something by folding it

create to make something no one else has made or can make

creator someone who makes what no one else has made or can make

creature any animal

creek a small stream

creep **1** to move along, keeping close to the ground
2 to move quietly or secretly
We **crept** away and nobody saw us.

crêpe paper (say krape paper)
thin, coloured paper that you can stretch

crept see **creep**

crescent a street shaped like a curved line

cress a small, green plant that is eaten raw

crew a group of people who work together on a boat or aeroplane

crib a baby's bed with bars round it to stop the baby falling out

cricket **1** a game played in a field by two teams with a ball, two bats, and two wickets
2 an insect that makes a

shrill sound by rubbing its front wings together

cried see **cry**

crime a bad deed that breaks the law

criminal someone who has done something bad that breaks the law

crimson a deep red colour

crinkle to make small lines in skin or paper by creasing it

cripple someone whose legs or arms are hurt so that he cannot use them properly

crisp 1 very dry so that it breaks easily
2 firm and fresh
*a very **crisp** apple*
3 a very thin, dry slice of fried potato

criss-cross with lines that cross each other

croak to make the hoarse sound a frog makes

crocodile a large animal that lives in rivers in some hot countries. It has short legs, a long body, and sharp teeth.

crocus a small white, yellow, or purple spring flower

crook 1 someone who cheats or robs people

2 a shepherd's stick with a curved top

crooked not straight

crop 1 plants grown on a farm for food
2 to bite off the tops of plants. Sheep crop grass.

cross 1 to move across something
2 a mark like this + or ×
3 the shape of + or ×
4 angry

crouch to lean forwards and bend your knees so that your bottom is almost touching the ground

crow a big, black bird

crowd a large number of people

crown a big ring of silver or gold worn on the head by a king or queen

cruel very unkind

cruise to sail without hurrying

crumb a tiny bit of bread or cake

crumble to break or fall into small pieces

crumple to make something very creased
crumpled clothes

crunch to eat with the noise

you make when you eat
crisps

crush to damage something
by pressing it hard

crust the hard part round the
outside of bread

crutch a wooden stick that a
crippled person can lean on
when he is walking. It fits
under the top of his arm.
a pair of **crutches**

cry **1** to let tears fall from
your eyes
He was so upset that he
cried*.*
2 to shout

crystal a hard material like
very bright glass

cub a young bear, lion, tiger,
or wolf

Cub Scout a junior Scout

cube the shape of dice or
sugar lumps. Cubes have six
square sides that are all the
same size. (See the list of
shapes on page 249.)

cuckoo a bird that lays its
eggs in other birds' nests.
The male cry sounds like
cuck-oo.

cucumber a long, green
vegetable eaten raw

cuddle to put your arms

closely round a person or
animal that you love

cuff the part joined to the end
of a sleeve to fit round the
wrist

cul-de-sac a street closed at
one end

culprit the person who is
guilty

cunning crafty

cupboard a piece of furniture
or a space inside a wall.
Cupboards have doors and
usually some shelves.

cure to make well again

curiosity a wish to find out
about things

curious **1** wanting to know
about something
2 unusual
a **curious** *smell*

curl **1** a piece of hair twisted
into rings
2 ***to curl up*** to sit or lie
comfortably with the body
bent round itself

currant a small, black, dried
grape

current water, air, or electricity
moving in one direction

curry food cooked with a
yellow powder that gives it a
very strong flavour

curtain a piece of cloth pulled in front of a window or stage to cover it

curtsy to put one foot behind the other and bend the knees. Women and girls curtsy.
*She **curtsied** to the Queen.*

curve a line that is bent smoothly like the letter C

cushion a cloth bag filled with soft material so that it is comfortable to sit on or rest against

custard a thick, sweet, yellow liquid poured over puddings

custom something that is usually done. It is a custom to give Christmas presents.

customer someone who uses a shop or a bank

cut **1** to use scissors or a knife to open, divide, or shape something
*She's **cutting** out the picture.*
*I've **cut** up your meat for you.*
2 an opening in the skin made by something sharp

cutlery knives, forks, and spoons

cycle to ride a bicycle

cygnet (*say* sig-nit) a young swan

cylinder the shape of a tin of soup or a toilet roll (see the list of shapes on page 249)

cymbals a musical instrument that is two round pieces of metal that you bang together
*a pair of **cymbals***

cypress a kind of tree. It has dark leaves that it keeps all through the year.

Dd

dachshund (*say* daksund) a kind of dog with very short legs and a long body

daffodil a yellow flower that grows from a bulb

daft silly
*a **daft** idea*

dagger a very short sword with two sharp edges

daily every day
*a **daily** paper*

55

dairy **1** a place where milk is made into butter and cheese **2** a shop that sells milk, cream, butter, and cheese

daisy a small flower with white petals and a yellow centre

dale a valley

dam a wall built to hold water back. Some dams are built to stop floods happening.

damage to harm something

damp a little wet
damp grass

damson a small, dark purple plum

dance to move about in time to music

dandelion a yellow wild flower with a thick stalk

danger **1** something that is dangerous **2** the chance of something dangerous happening
danger of fire

dangerous likely to kill or harm you
It's *dangerous* to play in the road.

dangle to hang loosely

dare **1** to be brave enough or rude enough to do something
I *daren't* dive in. How *dare* you!

2 to ask someone to show how brave he is
I *dare* you to climb that tree.

daring very brave

dark **1** without any light
a *dark* house
2 not light in colour
a *dark* green coat

darling someone who is loved very much

darn to sew over a hole in a garment to mend it

dart **1** to move very quickly and suddenly **2** a kind of short arrow that you throw

dash **1** to move very quickly **2** a mark like this —

date **1** the day, the month, and the year when something happens **2** a sweet, brown fruit that grows on a palm tree

daughter a girl or woman who is someone's child

dawdle to walk too slowly

dawn the time of the day when the sun rises

day **1** the twenty-four hours between midnight and the next midnight **2** the part of the day when it is light

dazed not able to think properly. People are often dazed after an accident.

dazzle to be so bright that it hurts your eyes to look
*The sun was **dazzling**.*

dead not alive

deaf not able to hear

deal 1 to give out
*I **dealt** the cards last time.*
2 to deal with something to do a job that needs doing
3 a great deal a lot

dealt (*say* delt)
see **deal**

dear 1 loved. Dear is always used to begin letters, for example
***Dear** Uncle Tom . . .*
2 costing a lot
*butter is **dear***

death the end of life

debt something that you owe someone

decay to go bad
*Sugar makes teeth **decay**.*

deceit making someone believe something that is not true

deceive to make someone believe something that is not true

decide to make up your mind about something

decimal 1 using tens
*the **decimal** system*
2 a way of writing fractions by putting numbers after a dot
$\frac{3}{10}$ is 0.3 $1\frac{1}{2}$ is 1.5

decision what you have decided

deck a floor on a ship or bus

declare to say something important that you want everyone to know

decorate to make something look pretty

decrease to make smaller or fewer

deed something special that someone has done
*a good **deed***

deep going a long way down from the top
***deep** water, a **deep** hole*

deer a graceful animal that

can move very quickly. Male deer have big bones like branches growing out of their heads.
*two **deer***

defeat to beat someone in a game or battle

defend to keep someone or something safe from attack

definite fixed or certain
*a **definite** date for the holiday*

defy to say or show that you will not obey

degree a measurement for temperature. You can write it like this °, and so ten degrees is 10°.

delay **1** to make someone or something late
2 to put off doing something until later

deliberate done on purpose
*a **deliberate** mistake*

delicate **1** soft and fine
__delicate__ material
2 likely to get ill or damaged
*a **delicate** child*
__delicate__ machinery

delicious tasting or smelling very pleasant

delight to please very much

deliver **1** to bring things like

milk or newspapers to someone's house
2 to set free

delivery delivering something

demand to ask for something that you think you ought to get

demolish to knock something down and break it up
*a **demolished** house*

demonstrate to show
*She's **demonstrating** how it works.*

demonstration a lot of people marching through the streets to show everyone what they think about something

dense thick
*a **dense** fog, a **dense** forest*

dent to make a hollow in something hard, by hitting it. Cars are often dented in accidents.

dentist someone whose job is to look after teeth. He can take out bad teeth or fill them.

deny to say that something is not true

depart to go away

depend to trust someone or

something to give you the help you need
*The blind man **depends** on his guide dog.*

depress to make someone feel sad

depth how deep something is

descend (*say* dis-send) to go down

describe to say what something or someone is like

description words that tell you about someone or something

desert (*say* <u>dez</u>-ert) a very dry area of land where few plants can grow

deserted left by everyone
*a **deserted** house*

deserve to have done something that makes people think you should get a reward or a punishment
*He was so brave he **deserves** a medal.*

design to draw a plan or pattern for something

desire to want very much

desk a kind of table where you can read, write, and keep books

despair to give up hope

desperate ready to do even dangerous or stupid things, because you have lost hope
*a **desperate** robber*

despise to dislike someone because he is bad and you think you are much better than he is
*They **despised** him because he had cheated.*

dessert (*say* diz-<u>ert</u>) sweet food eaten after the main part of a meal

destination the place you are travelling to

destroy **1** to damage something so badly that it cannot be used again **2** to kill a very sick animal that cannot be cured

destroyer a small, fast ship for attacking other ships

destruction when something is destroyed

detail a tiny piece of information about something

detective someone who tries to find out who did a murder or robbery

determined with your mind firmly made up
determined to win

detest to hate

develop to become bigger or better

dew tiny drops of water that come during the night on things outside

diagonal a slanting line drawn from one corner of something to the opposite corner (see page 249)

diagram a kind of picture that explains something

dial a circle with numbers or letters round it. Clocks, watches, and telephones have dials.

dialect the way people living in a particular place speak

diameter a straight line drawn across a circle, through the centre (see page 248)

diamond **1** a very hard jewel like clear glass

2 a shape with four sloping sides that are the same length. Some playing-cards have red diamonds printed on them.

diary a book where you can write down what happens every day

dice more than one **die**

dictionary (*say* dik-shun-ree) a book where you can find out what a word means and how to spell it

did see **do**

die **1** to stop living
*The dog was **dying**.*
*The king has **died**.*
2 a small cube used in games. Each side is marked with a different number of spots from 1 to 6.
*two **dice***

diesel (*rhymes with* weasel) an engine that burns oil to make power

diet special meals that some people must have to be healthy

difference how different one thing is from another thing

different not like someone or something else

difficult not easy
*a **difficult** sum*

difficulty 1 something difficult
2 **with difficulty** not easily

dig to move soil away to make a hole in the ground
*I **dug** a hole and planted the tree.*

digest to change the food in your stomach so that your body can use it

dignified looking serious and important

dim not bright

dimple a small hollow in the cheek or chin

dinghy (*say* ding-ee) a small boat

dingy (*say* din-jee) looking dirty
*a **dingy** room*

dining-room the room where people have their meals

dinner the main meal of the day

dinosaur a large animal that lived on the land millions of years ago

direct 1 to show someone the way
2 as straight and quick as it can be
*the **direct** route*

direction the way you go to get somewhere

dirt dust or mud

dirty marked with dirt or stains
*a **dirty** face*

disagree to think that someone else is wrong and you are right

disappear to go away and not be seen any more

disappoint to make someone sad by not doing what he hoped

disaster something very bad that happens suddenly

disciple one of the first followers of Jesus Christ

discourage to try to stop someone doing something by telling him how difficult it is

discover to find out about something

discovery finding out about something

discuss to talk about something with people who have different ideas about it

disease any illness

disgraceful so bad that it brings you shame
disgraceful work

disguise to make yourself look different so that people will not recognize you
*The thief **disguised** himself as a policeman.*

disgust to be so nasty that people hate it

dish a shallow bowl

dishonest not honest

dislike the feeling you have for someone or something you do not like

dismal dark and sad

dismay to make someone lose hope and be afraid

dismiss to send someone away

display **1** to show
2 a show
*a dancing **display***

dissolve to mix something into a liquid so that it becomes part of the liquid. You can dissolve salt in water very easily.

distance the amount of space between two places

distant far away

distinct **1** easy to see or hear
2 different

distress great sorrow, trouble, or worry

district part of a town, city, county, or country

disturb **1** to upset someone's peace or rest
2 to move something out of place

disturbance something that upsets someone's peace or rest

ditch a long, narrow hole. Ditches are dug to take away water from land.

divan a low bed

dive to jump head first into water

divide **1** to share something out
2 to split something into smaller parts
3 to find out how many times one number goes into another. Six divided by two is three, $6 \div 2 = 3$.

dizzy feeling as if everything is spinning round you

do **1** to carry out an action
She **does** her sewing neatly. **Don't** cry. What are you **doing**?
2 to finish
I **did** my work before I went out to play. He **didn't**. Have you **done** your picture yet?

dock a place where ships and boats are loaded, unloaded, or mended

doctor someone whose job is to help sick people to get better

dodge to move quickly to get out of the way of something

doe a female deer, rabbit, or hare

does see **do**

doll a toy in the shape of a person

dollar an amount of money. Dollars are used in the United States of America, Australia, and some other countries.

dolphin an animal with warm blood that lives in the sea

dome a roof shaped like the top half of a ball. St Paul's Cathedral has a dome.

domino a small, oblong piece of wood or plastic with spots on it. You use twenty-eight dominoes to play the game called **dominoes**.

done see **do**

donkey an animal that looks like a small horse with long ears

doodle to scribble while you are thinking about something else

door a tall piece of wood that fills an opening in a wall. You can open a door to get into or out of a place.

dose the amount of medicine someone has to take

double twice as much or as many

doubt (rhymes with out) the feeling you have when

you are not sure about something

doubtful not sure

dough (*rhymes with* so) a mixture of flour and water. Dough is used for making bread and cakes.

doughnut a small cake that is fried and covered in sugar

dove a bird that looks like a small pigeon

down 1 to somewhere lower *Run **down** the hill.* 2 very soft feathers

downward, downwards moving to somewhere lower

doze to be nearly asleep

dozen a set of twelve

drab looking dull ***drab** clothes*

drag to pull something heavy along

dragon a monster with wings, that you read about in stories. Dragons breathe out fire and often guard treasure.

dragonfly a brightly coloured insect that lives near water

drain 1 a pipe for taking away water 2 to get rid of water by using pipes or ditches

drake a male duck

drama acting in a play or story

drank see **drink**

draught (*rhymes with* raft) 1 cold air that blows into a room 2 one of twenty-four round pieces used in the game of **draughts**

draw 1 to do a picture with a pen, pencil, or crayon *It was **drawn** in crayon.* 2 to end a game with the same score as the other side *They **drew** 1–1 last Saturday.*

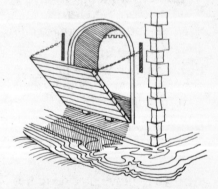

drawbridge a bridge over the water round a castle. It can be pulled up to stop people getting into the castle.

drawer a box without a lid, that slides into a piece of furniture

drawn see **draw**

dread great fear

dreadful very bad
  dreadful weather

dream to see and hear things while you are asleep
  Last night I **dreamt** about Christmas.

drench to make someone very wet all over
  He was **drenched** by the rain.

dress 1 to put clothes on
  2 a piece of clothing that is like a skirt and blouse in one

drew see **draw**

dribble 1 to let liquid come out of your mouth without meaning to. Babies often dribble.
  2 to keep kicking a ball as you run along, so that the ball stays close to your feet

drift to be carried gently along by water or air

drill a tool for making holes

drink to swallow liquid
  Have you **drunk** your milk?
  He was thirsty so he **drank** a lot.

drip to let drops of liquid fall off

drive to make a machine or animal move
  He's never **driven** a bus before.
  I **drove** the cows into the field last night.
  He was **driving** too fast.

drizzle very light rain

droop to hang down weakly
  a **drooping** flower

drop 1 a tiny amount of liquid
  2 to let something fall

drove see **drive**

drown to die because you are under water and cannot breathe

drowsy sleepy

drum a hollow musical instrument that you bang with a stick

drunk see **drink**

dry not damp or wet
  dry land

duchess a woman married to a duke

duck 1 a bird that lives near water. It has a wide, flat beak.
  2 to bend down quickly to get out of the way

due 1 expected
  The train is **due** now.
  2 **due to** caused by

*The accident was **due to** the fog.*

duel a fight between two people using the same kind of weapon
*a **duel** with swords*

duffel-coat a thick coat with a hood and long, narrow buttons that go through loops

dug see **dig**

duke a very important nobleman

dull 1 not interesting
*a **dull** book*
2 not bright
*a **dull** colour*
3 not sharp
*a **dull** sound*

dumb not able to speak

dummy 1 a piece of rubber made for a baby to suck
2 a model of a person. You often see dummies in shop windows.

dump 1 a place where rubbish is left
2 to leave something you want to get rid of
3 to put something down carelessly

dungeon (*say* dunjun)
a prison underneath a building

during while something else is going on
*I fell asleep **during** the film.*

dusk the dim light at the end of the day, before it gets dark

dust 1 dry dirt that is like powder
2 to clear dust away from something

dustbin a large container with a lid, for rubbish

duty what you ought to do

duvet a large, cloth bag filled with something soft like feathers and used instead of sheets and blankets on a bed

dwarf someone who is very small

dwindle to get smaller and smaller

dye to change the colour of something by putting it in a special liquid

dying see **die**

dynamite something very powerful that is used for blowing things up
*a stick of **dynamite***

Ee

each every
Each child had a cake.

eager full of a strong wish to do something

eagle a large bird that eats other animals

ear **1** the part of the head used for hearing
2 the group of seeds at the top of a stalk of corn

early **1** near the beginning
early in the day
2 sooner than was expected
She came *early*.

earn to get money by working for it

earth **1** the planet that we all live on
2 soil

earthquake a time when the ground suddenly shakes.
Strong earthquakes can destroy buildings.

ease rest from pain and trouble

easel a stand for holding a blackboard or a picture while you work at it

east in the direction of the rising sun

Easter the day when people specially remember that Jesus Christ came back from the dead

eastern from the east or in the east

easy **1** able to be done or understood without any trouble
an *easy* sum
2 comfortable
an *easy* chair

eat to take food into the body
Has he *eaten* his dinner?
He *ate* it all five minutes ago.

ebb the movement of the sea back from the land

eccentric likely to behave in a strange way

echo a sound that is heard again as it bounces back off something solid. Echoes are often heard in caves and tunnels.

eclipse **1** a time when the moon comes between the earth and the sun so that the sun's light cannot be seen
2 a time when the earth comes between the sun and the moon so that the moon's light cannot be seen

edge the part along the end or side of something

editor the person in charge of a newspaper, magazine, or comic. Editors decide which stories and pictures should be printed.

education the teaching and training people get in schools and colleges

eel a fish that looks like a snake

effect anything that happens because of something else

effort hard work at something you are trying to do

egg **1** a round object with a thin shell, made by a hen and used as food
2 one of the round objects that baby birds, fish, insects, or snakes live inside until they are big enough to be born

eiderdown a large, cloth bag filled with something soft like feathers and used as a cover for a bed

either one or the other of two people or things
It's **either** right or wrong.

elastic a strip of material that can stretch in length and then go back to its usual size

elbow the bony part in the middle of the arm where it bends

elder older than another person

election a time when people can choose the men and women who will be in charge of their town or country
a General **Election**

electric worked by electricity

electricity power that moves along wires. Electricity is used for giving light and heat and for making machines work.

elephant a very big grey animal with tusks and a very long nose called a trunk, that it uses like an arm

elf a kind of naughty fairy
two **elves**

elm a kind of tall tree

else besides
*Ask someone **else**.*

embark to get on a ship at the beginning of a journey

embarrass to make someone feel shy and upset

embrace to put your arms round someone

embroidery pretty sewing that decorates something

emerald a green jewel

emergency something very dangerous that suddenly happens

emigrate to go and live in another country

emperor a man who rules over a group of countries

empire a group of countries ruled over by one person

employ to pay someone to work for you

empress **1** a woman who rules over a group of countries
2 the wife of an emperor

empty with nothing in it or on it

enamel **1** a kind of paint that gives a hard, shiny surface to things
2 the hard, shiny surface of your teeth

encourage to make someone brave and full of hope so that he will do something

encyclopedia a book or a set of books that tells you about all kinds of things

end **1** the last part of something
2 to finish

endeavour to try hard

enemy **1** someone who wants to hurt you
2 the people fighting on the other side

energetic full of the strength for doing a lot of things

energy the strength to do things

engine a machine that makes its own power and is used to make things move

engineer someone who plans the building of roads, bridges, or machines

enjoy to like watching, listening to, or doing something

enormous very big

enough not less than is needed
enough money

enter **1** to come or go in

69

2 to take part in a race or a competition

entertain to make time pass very pleasantly for people

entertainment anything that entertains people. Shows, circuses, plays, and films are entertainments.

enthusiasm a very great interest in something
an **enthusiasm** for football

enthusiastic so interested in something that you spend a lot of time on it and are always talking about it

entire whole
The **entire** class was ill.

entrance the way into a place

entry 1 a way into a place
2 going or coming into a place
3 a person, animal, or thing in a competition

envelope a paper cover for a letter

envious full of envy

envy a feeling you get when you would like to have something that someone else has

equal the same as something else in amount, size, or value

equal shares

equator an imaginary line round the middle of the earth. Countries near the equator are very hot.

equipment the things you need for doing something

erect upright

errand a short journey to take a message or fetch something for someone

error a mistake

escalator a moving staircase

escape 1 to get free
2 to get away

Eskimo one of the people who live in very cold parts of North America, Greenland, and Russia

especially more than anything else

estate 1 an area of land with a lot of houses on it
2 a large area of land that belongs to one person

estimate to guess the amount, size, or price

eve the day or night before a special day
Christmas **Eve**

even 1 level or equal
Our scores were **even**.

2 that two will go into
*Six is an **even** number.*

evening the time at the end of the day before people go to bed

event something important that happens

eventually in the end

ever **1** at any time
*Have you **ever** read this?*
2 *for ever* always

evergreen any tree that has green leaves all through the year

every each
***Every** week has seven days.*

everybody, everyone every person

everything all things

everywhere in all places

evil very wicked
*an **evil** deed*

ewe (*say* you)
a female sheep

exact just right

exaggerate to make something sound bigger than it is

exam, examination an important test

examine to look at something very carefully

example **1** anything that shows how something works or what it is like
2 a person or thing that should be copied

excellent very good

except apart from
*Everyone got a prize **except** me.*

exchange to give something and get something in return

excite to interest someone so much that he has strong feelings such as love, fear, or anger
*an **exciting** film*

excitement an excited feeling

exclaim to make a sudden sound because you are surprised or excited

exclamation mark a mark like this ! put after words to show that they have been shouted

excursion a trip out somewhere for the day or afternoon
*an **excursion** to the seaside*

excuse[1] *(ends in the sound — s)*
words that try to explain why you have done wrong so that you will not get into trouble

71

excuse² (*ends in the sound —z*)
to forgive

execute to kill someone as a punishment

exercise **1** work that makes your body healthy and strong
2 a piece of work that you do to make yourself better at something

exhausted tired out

exhibition a group of things put on show so that people can come to see them

exile someone who has to live away from his own country

exist **1** to be real, not imaginary
Do fairies **exist**?
2 to live

exit the way out of a place

expand to get bigger

expect to think something is very likely to happen

expedition a journey made in order to do something
a climbing **expedition**

expensive with a high price
an **expensive** *car*

experience **1** what you have learnt from things that you have seen and done

2 something that has happened to you

experiment a test to find out whether an idea works

expert someone who does something very well or knows a lot about something

explain to make something clear to people so that they understand it

explanation something said or written to help people to understand

explode to make something burst or blow up with a loud bang

explore to look carefully round a place for the first time

explosion a loud bang made by something bursting or blowing up

explosive anything used for making things blow up

express **1** a fast train
2 to put an idea or feeling into words

expression the look on someone's face

extension a part that has been added to make something bigger

extent the length or area of something

extinguish to put out a fire

extra more than usual

extraordinary very unusual

extravagant always ready to spend much more money than people think you ought

extreme 1 very great
extreme cold
2 the furthest away
the *extreme* north

eye 1 the part of the head used for seeing
2 the small hole in a needle

eyebrow the curved line of hair above each eye

eyelash one of the short hairs that grow in a fringe around each eye

Ff

fable a story about animals that teaches people something

face 1 the front part of the head
2 a surface
A cube has six *faces*.
3 to have the front towards something

The church is *facing* the school.

fact anything that people know is true

factory a building where machines are used to make things

fade 1 to lose colour
faded curtains
2 to get paler or quieter so that it is harder to see or hear

Fahrenheit (*say* farren-hite) a way of measuring temperature that gives 32 degrees for freezing water and 212 degrees for boiling water

fail to try to do something but not be able to do it

failure someone or something that has failed

faint 1 weak
a *faint* cry
2 to feel so dizzy that everything goes black and you fall down

fair 1 light in colour
fair hair
2 right or just
It's not *fair*.
3 a group of roundabouts, stalls, shows, and games that come together in a place for a few days

fairly 1 without cheating
*Play **fairly**.*
2 almost or quite
***fairly** good*
*I'm **fairly** sure.*

fairy one of the tiny, magic
people in stories

faith belief in someone or
something

faithful always ready to help
your friends and do what you
have promised to do

fake something not valuable
that is made to look valuable

fall to come down suddenly
*He's **fallen** off his bike.*
*I **fell** over yesterday.*

false 1 not real
***false** teeth*
2 not true
*a **false** friend*

falter 1 to keep stopping and
nearly falling over
2 to keep stopping while you
are speaking

fame being famous
*great **fame***

familiar well known to you
*a **familiar** face*

family parents and their
children and grandchildren

famine a time when there is
very little food

famous very well known

fancy 1 decorated
*a **fancy** hat*
2 fancy dress unusual
dressing-up clothes
3 to want
*I **fancied** an ice-cream.*

fang a long, sharp tooth
*Dogs, wolves, and poisonous
snakes have fangs.*

far a long way
***far** from home*

fare the money people have to
pay to travel on trains,
buses, boats, or aeroplanes

farewell goodbye

farm a piece of land where
someone grows crops and
keeps animals for food

farmer someone who keeps a
farm

farther to a greater distance
*I live **farther** away now.*

fashion the way of dressing
most people like to try and
copy

fast 1 moving quickly
*a **fast** car*
2 quickly
*Don't drive too **fast**.*
3 firmly fixed
*It was stuck **fast** in the mud.*
4 showing a time that is later
than the correct time.

Watches and clocks are
sometimes fast.
5 to go without food

fasten **1** to close something
so that it will not come open
2 to join something

fastener something used for
fastening things

fat **1** with a very thick, round
body
2 the white, greasy part of
meat
3 any grease that is used in
cooking. Butter, margarine,
and lard are fats.

fatal causing a person or
animal to die
a **fatal** accident

father a male parent

fault something wrong that
spoils a person or thing

favour something kind that
you do for someone

favourite liked the most

fawn **1** a young deer
2 a light brown colour

fear **1** a feeling you get when
you think something bad
might happen to you
2 to be afraid of someone or
something

feast a special meal for a lot
of people

feat something brave or
difficult that has been done

feather one of the many light,
flat parts that cover a bird
instead of hair or fur

fed see **feed**

feeble weak

feed **1** to give food to a
person or animal
I **fed** the cat last night.
2 to eat
The pigs are **feeding** now.

feel **1** to touch something to
find out what it is like
2 to know something inside
yourself
I **felt** sad yesterday.

feeling something that you
feel inside yourself, like
anger or love

feet more than one **foot**

fell see **fall**

felt **1** see **feel**
2 a kind of cloth made from
wool

female any person or animal
that can become a mother.
Women, girls, cows, and
hens are all females.

fence a kind of wall made of
wood or posts and wire.
Fences are put round
gardens and fields.

fender a metal bar put round a fire to stop pieces of coal from rolling into the room

fern a plant with leaves like feathers and no flowers

ferret a small animal used for catching rats and rabbits

ferry a boat that takes people from one side of a piece of water to the other

fertile able to make a lot of healthy plants
fertile soil

festival a time when people do special things to show that they are happy about something

fetch to go and get

fête (*rhymes with* date) a kind of party in the open air with competitions and stalls selling different things

fever an illness that makes people feel very hot and dizzy

few not many

fiddle 1 a violin
2 to play about with something

fidget to keep moving because you cannot keep still

field a piece of ground with a fence around it and crops or grass growing on it

fierce angry and cruel

fight to take part in a struggle, battle, or war
We ***fought*** *until it was dark.*

figure 1 one of the signs for numbers, such as 1, 2, and 3
2 the shape of a body

file 1 a line of people one behind the other
2 a flat tool that is rubbed against things to make them smooth

fill to make someone or something full

film 1 a piece or roll of thin plastic put in a camera for taking photographs
2 moving photographs with sound that tell a story

filthy very dirty

fin one of the thin, flat parts

that stand out from a fish's body and help it swim

find to come across something, either by chance or because you have been looking for it
I've **found** my coat.

fine **1** very thin
fine material
2 dry and sunny
fine weather
3 very good
a **fine** picture
4 money someone has to pay as a punishment

finger one of the five separate parts at the end of the hand

fingerprint the mark left on the surface of something by the tip of a finger

finish to come to the end of something

fir a tall tree that has cones and leaves that look like green needles

fire **1** the heat and bright light that come from burning things

2 **to fire a gun** to shoot

fireman a man whose job is to put out fires

fire-place the part of a room where the fire and hearth are

firework a paper tube filled with a powder that will burn noisily and bang or send out coloured sparks and smoke

firm fixed so that it will not give way

first before all the others

fish **1** any animal with scales and fins that always lives and breathes under water
2 to try to catch fish

fisherman someone who catches fish

fishmonger someone who keeps a shop that sells fish

fist a hand with all the fingers pressed in towards the palm

fit **1** healthy
2 good enough
fit for a king
3 to be the right size and shape

fix **1** to join firmly to something
2 to mend

fizzy with a lot of tiny bubbles that keep bursting
fizzy drinks

flag a piece of coloured cloth with a pattern on it, joined to a stick. Every country has its own flag.

flake a very thin, light piece of something
soap **flakes**

flame fire that is shaped like a pointed tongue

flannel a piece of soft cloth used for washing yourself

flap **1** to move up and down like a bird's wings
2 a part that hangs down and is joined to the rest by one side. Envelopes have flaps.

flare to burn with a sudden, bright flame

flash to shine suddenly and brightly

flask a container that keeps hot drinks hot and cold drinks cold

flat **1** not curved and with no bumps in it
2 a home that is a set of rooms inside a house or a big building

flatten to make flat

flatter to praise someone too much

flavour the smell and taste of something

flea a small insect without wings that sucks blood and jumps

flee to run away
He saw the policeman and **fled**.

fleece the wool that covers a sheep

flesh the soft stuff between the bones and skin

flew see **fly**

flight **1** a journey through the air
2 an escape
3 **a flight of stairs** a set of stairs

flinch to move back slightly because you are afraid

fling to throw something as hard as you can
I **flung** a stone and hit the giant.

float **1** to be on the top of a liquid
2 to be carried along by liquid or air

flock a group of birds or sheep that feed together

flood a lot of water that spreads over land that is usually dry

floor the part of a building or room that people walk on

flop to fall or sit down suddenly

flour a powder made from wheat and used for making bread, pastry, and cakes

flourish 1 to grow well 2 to be happy and successful

flow to move along like a river

flower the part of a plant that is pretty and not coloured green

flown see **fly**

flu an illness that gives you a cold and makes you ache all over and feel very hot

fluff light, soft stuff that comes off wool, hair, or feathers

fluid any liquid or gas

fluke a piece of luck that makes you able to do something you thought you could not do

flung see **fling**

flutter 1 to keep moving the wings quickly, but not fly very far 2 to move a little, like a flag in a very light wind

fly 1 to move through the air with wings or in an aeroplane *I **flew** from London to Paris last week.*
*He's never **flown** before.* 2 a small insect with one pair of wings *two **flies***

foal a young horse

foam 1 a lot of small bubbles on the top of a liquid 2 thick, soft rubber used for making sponges

fog damp air that looks like thick smoke and is difficult to see through

fold to lay one part of something on top of another part

folder a large cover made of card for keeping your work in

foliage leaves

folk people

follow to go after

fond liking someone or something a lot ***fond** of fish fingers*

food anything that you eat to help you grow and be healthy

fool someone who is very silly

foolish silly

foot 1 the part joined to the lower end of the leg *two **feet*** 2 a measure for length

football a game played by two teams who kick a ball and try to score goals

footprint the mark left by a foot

footsteps the sound your feet make as you walk or run

forbid to say that someone must not do something
*She was **forbidden** to go out.*

force **1** to use your power to make a person, animal, or thing do something
2 a group of people with weapons
3 power

forecast saying what you think is going to happen before it happens
*a weather **forecast***

forehead the part of the face above the eyebrows

foreign belonging to another country
***foreign** coins*

forest a lot of trees growing together

forgave see **forgive**

forge **1** to write or paint like someone else so that people will think he did it
2 to make a copy of something and pretend it is real

3 a place where metal is heated and shaped

forgery writing or a picture that is made to look as if someone else has done it

forget to fail to remember
*I've **forgotten** my dinner money.*
*I **forgot** the time and was late.*

forgive to stop being angry with someone
*Have you **forgiven** me?*
*I **forgave** him when he explained.*

forgot, forgotten see **forget**

fork a tool with three or four thin pointed parts. People use small forks for picking up food and putting it into their mouths.

form **1** the shape something has
2 a long wooden seat without a back
3 one of the classes in a school
4 a printed paper with spaces where you have to write

fort a strong building with soldiers in it, made to protect a place against its enemies

fortnight two weeks

fortress a big fort

fortunate lucky

fortune **1** a lot of money
2 luck

forward, forwards in the direction you are facing

fossil any part of a dead plant or animal that has been in the ground millions of years and become hard like rock

foster-mother a woman who takes a child to live with her family while his own parents cannot look after him

fought see **fight**

foul dirty and bad

found see **find**

foundations the solid part under the ground that a building is built on

fountain water that shoots up into the air

fowl any bird that is kept for its meat or eggs

fox a wild animal that looks like a dog and has a long, furry tail

fraction **1** a number that is not a whole number. $\frac{1}{2}$, $\frac{3}{5}$, and $\frac{1}{4}$ are fractions.
2 a very small part of something

fragile easily broken

fragment a small piece that has been broken off
fragments of rock

frame **1** something that fits round the edge of a picture
2 a set of parts that fit together to give something its shape

fraud a trick or a person who tries to cheat someone

freak any person, animal, or thing with something very strange about it

freckle one of the small brown spots people sometimes get on their skin, when they have been in the sun

free **1** with nothing to stop you doing something or going somewhere
2 not costing anything
a **free** gift

freeze **1** to change into ice
The pond **froze** last night.
2 to be very cold
Your hands will be **frozen**.

frequent happening often
frequent rain

fresh **1** not old, tired, or used
fresh air, **fresh** bread
a **fresh** start
2 not tinned
fresh fruit

fret to keep worrying and getting upset about something

fridge short for **refrigerator**

friend someone you like who likes you. Friends like doing things together.

frieze a wide strip of pictures along the top of a wall

fright sudden fear

frighten to make someone afraid

frill a strip of material with tiny pleats in it. Frills are stitched to the edges of things to decorate them.

fringe **1** short hair brushed forward on to the forehead **2** a band of material with loose threads hanging from it, put round the edges of things to decorate them

fritter a slice of potato, fruit, or meat dipped in a mixture of egg, flour, and milk and fried

frog a small animal with a smooth, wet skin. Frogs live near water and jump.

from out of

front the side that people usually see or come to first

frost ice that looks like powder and covers things when the weather is very cold

froth a lot of small bubbles on the top of a liquid

frown to have lines on your forehead because you are angry or worried

froze, frozen see **freeze**

fruit the seed of a plant and the soft or juicy part round it

fry to cook in hot fat in a pan on top of a stove

frying-pan a large, shallow pan

fudge a kind of soft, very sweet toffee

fuel anything that is burnt to make heat

full with no more room

fund money that will be used for something special

funeral the time when a dead person's body is buried or burnt

fungus a kind of plant that is not green and grows in damp places. Mushrooms and toadstools are both **fungi**.

funnel **1** a chimney on a ship or railway engine

2 a tube with one very wide end to help you pour things into bottles

funny **1** amusing
*a very **funny** joke*
2 strange
*a **funny** smell*

fur the soft hair that covers some animals

furious very angry

furniture things such as beds and tables that you need inside a house and can move about

furrow the straight, narrow hollow made in the ground by a plough

furry covered in fur

further to a greater distance
*I swam **further** than you.*

fuse **1** a piece of cord used for setting off an explosion
2 a small piece of wire that will melt to stop too much

electricity going through. Most plugs have fuses in them.

fuss to worry and bother too much about something that is not important

future the time that will come

Gg

gabble to talk so quickly that it is difficult for other people to understand what you are saying

gadget a small, useful tool

gain to get something that you did not have before

galaxy a very large group of stars that belong together, such as the Milky Way

gale a very strong wind

galleon a Spanish ship with sails, used long ago

gallery 1 a building or long room where paintings are shown
*an art **gallery***
2 the upstairs seats in a theatre or church

galley 1 a large boat used long ago that needed a lot of men to row it
2 the kitchen on a ship

gallon a measure for liquid

gallop to move like a horse moving very quickly

gamble to try to win money by playing a game that needs luck

game something that you play at that has rules. Football and draughts are games.

gander a male goose

gang 1 a group of people who do things together
2 a group of criminals who work together

gangster someone who belongs to a gang that robs and kills people

gangway 1 the plank or set of steps that people walk up to get on to a boat
2 the path between rows of seats in a large building

gaol (*say* jail)
prison

gape 1 to have your mouth wide open with surprise
2 to be wide open

garage 1 the building where a car or bus is kept
2 a place that sells petrol and mends cars

garden a piece of ground where flowers, fruit, or vegetables are grown

gargle to wash your throat by moving liquid around inside it

garment a piece of clothing

garter a band of elastic put round a sock to keep it up

gas 1 anything that is like air. Some gases have strong smells.
2 a gas that is burnt to make heat

gash a deep cut

gasp to breathe in noisily and quickly because you are surprised or ill

gate a kind of door in a wall or fence round a piece of land

gather **1** to bring together **2** to pick

gave see **give**

gay **1** cheerful
*a **gay** tune*
2 brightly coloured
***gay** curtains*

gaze to look at something for a long time

gear **1** the things needed for a job or sport
*camping **gear***
2 part of a bicycle or car. Gears help to control the speed of the wheels so that it is easier to go up and down hills.

geese more than one **goose**

gem a valuable or beautiful stone

general **1** belonging to most people or things
2 an important officer in the army

generous always ready to give or share what you have

gentle quiet and kind

gentleman a polite name for a man
*Ladies and **gentlemen** ...*

genuine real
*Is that diamond **genuine**?*

geography finding out about different parts of the world

geranium a plant with red, pink, or white flowers that is often grown in a pot

gerbil (*begins with the sound* j—)
a small, pale brown animal with long back legs and very soft fur. Gerbils dig holes in sand and are often kept as pets.

germ something that is alive but too small to see and helps to make people ill

get **1** to become
2 to take, buy, or be given something
*I **got** a new bike yesterday. I'm **getting** one for my birthday.*

ghost the shape of a dead person that people think they have seen moving as if he were alive

giant one of the very big people in fairy stories

giddy dizzy

gift a present

gigantic (*say* jy-gantic) very big

giggle to keep laughing in a silly way because you cannot stop yourself

gill the part on each side of a fish that it breathes through

ginger a powder that gives a strong, hot taste to sweet things

gingerbread sticky cake or thick biscuit that tastes of ginger

gipsy one of a group of people with dark hair and skin, who do not live in houses but travel from place to place in caravans

giraffe a very tall African animal with a very long neck

girl **1** a female child or teenager
2 a young woman

give to let someone have something
Dad **gave** me this yesterday.
She was **given** first prize.
I'm **giving** you a second chance.

glacier a river of ice that moves very slowly down a mountain

glad happy

glance to look at something quickly

glare **1** to look angrily at someone
2 a very strong light

glass **1** something hard that you can see through. Glass is used for making windows.
2 a kind of cup that is made of glass and has no handle

glasses a pair of glass lenses held in front of the eyes by a frame that fits over the nose and ears. People wear glasses to help them to see better.

gleam to shine with a soft light

glen a narrow valley in Scotland and Ireland

glide to move very smoothly

glider a kind of aeroplane without an engine

glimmer a very weak light

glimpse to see something for only a few seconds

glint to shine with a bright light that comes and goes. Gold glints.

glisten to shine like something with drops of water on it

glitter to shine with a bright light that keeps coming and going *glittering* jewels

globe a ball with the map of the whole world on it

gloomy **1** dark
*a **gloomy** room*
2 sad
*a **gloomy** face*

glory **1** great fame
2 great beauty

glossy smooth and shiny

glove a covering for the hand with separate parts for the thumb and each finger

glow to shine with the warm light a fire has

glue a thick liquid for sticking things together

glum not pleased or happy
*He looked **glum**.*

glutton someone who eats too much

gnarled (*say* narled)
twisted like the trunk of an old tree

gnat (*say* nat)
a thin fly that sucks blood

gnaw (*say* nor)
to keep biting something hard like a bone

gnome (*say* nome)
a kind of ugly fairy

go to move in any direction

*His car **goes** very fast.*
*She's **gone** out to play.*
*They **went** on holiday yesterday.*
*When are you **going**?*

goal **1** the two posts the ball must go between to score a point in games like football
2 a point scored in football, netball, and other games

goat an animal kept for its meat and milk. Goats often have a strong smell.

gobble to eat very quickly and greedily

goblin a kind of bad, ugly fairy

goes see **go**

go-kart a kind of small, simple racing car

gold a valuable, shiny, yellow metal

golden coloured like gold

goldfish a small orange fish often kept as a pet

golf a game played by hitting small, white balls with sticks called clubs, over a large area of ground

gone see **go**

good **1** of the kind people like and praise
***good** work*
2 kind and true

a **good** friend
3 well behaved
a **good** boy

goodbye the word you say when you are leaving someone

goods things that can be bought and sold

goose a large bird that is kept for its meat and eggs
two **geese**

gooseberry a green berry that grows on a bush with thorns and can be cooked and eaten

gorgeous **1** very attractive **2** with bright colours

gorilla an African animal like a very large monkey with long arms and no tail

gorse a prickly bush with small yellow flowers

gosling a young goose

gossip **1** to talk a lot in a friendly way to someone **2** to talk a lot about other people

got see **get**

govern to be in charge of a place and decide what should happen there

government the group of people who are in charge of what happens in a country

grab to take hold of something suddenly

grace **1** beauty in the way someone moves or stands **2** a short prayer before or after a meal

gradual happening a little at a time
a **gradual** change

grain seed that grows in plants like corn and is used for making food

gramme a tiny measure for weight
1,000 **grammes** = 1 kilogramme

grand large, important, or wonderful

grandchild the child of a son or daughter
Granddaughters and **grandsons** are grandchildren.

grandfather the father of a father or mother

grandmother the mother of a father or mother

granite a very hard rock

grant to agree to give someone what he has asked for

grape a small, soft green or

purple fruit that grows in bunches

grapefruit a fruit that looks like a big orange, but is yellow

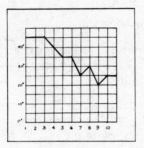

graph a diagram that helps you to see how numbers or amounts of things are different from each other

grasp to get hold of something and hold it tightly

grass a green plant with flat, narrow leaves that can be eaten by cattle and other animals

grasshopper an insect that makes a shrill sound by rubbing one leg against a wing and can jump a long way

grate **1** a container made of metal bars. Grates hold the coal or wood in a fire.
2 to rub something against a rough surface so that it falls into tiny pieces
3 to make the kind of noise the nail on your finger makes if you rub it against a blackboard

grateful full of a wish to thank someone for what he has done

grave **1** the hole in which a dead person is buried
2 very serious

gravel a mixture of sand and tiny stones

gravity the force that pulls everything towards the earth. If there was no gravity everyone would fall off the earth and float out into space.

gravy a hot brown liquid that is poured over meat before it is eaten

graze **1** to hurt the skin by rubbing hard against something
2 to eat grass as it grows. Cows and sheep graze in fields.

grease thick, slippery stuff like oil

great **1** large
*a **great** amount of money*
2 important
*a **great** man*

3 very good
*a **great** idea*

greed a wish for much more food or money than you really need

greengrocer someone who keeps a shop that sells fruit and vegetables

greenhouse a glass building for growing plants in

greet to welcome someone or say hello

grew see **grow**

grief a very sad feeling

grill to cook food on metal bars put under or over heat
*a **grilled** chop*

grim **1** not looking kind, friendly, or pleased
*a **grim** face*
2 not pleasant
grim weather

grin a smile that shows the teeth

grind to crush into tiny bits
*The wheat was **ground** into flour.*

grip to hold tightly

grit tiny bits of stone or sand

groan to make a low sound because you are in pain or trouble

grocer someone who keeps a shop that sells food, drink, and things like soap powder and matches

groom **1** someone whose job is to look after horses
2 to make an animal look smart by cleaning and brushing it

groove a long, narrow hollow. Records have grooves in them.

grope to try to find something by feeling for it when you cannot see

gross twelve dozen or 144

ground **1** the earth
2 a piece of land
3 see **grind**

group a number of people, animals, or things that belong together in some way

grow **1** to become bigger
*You've **grown** very quickly.*
2 to plant something in the ground and look after it
*We **grew** huge leeks last year.*

growl to make a deep, angry sound. Angry dogs growl.

grown see **grow**

grub a tiny creature that will become an insect

grudge a bad feeling you have against someone, because you think he has harmed you

gruff with a deep, rough voice

grumble to keep on saying that you are not pleased about something
Stop ***grumbling****!*

grunt to make the sound a pig makes

guard to keep someone or something safe from other people

guardian someone who is put in charge of a child whose parents cannot look after him

guess to say what you think the answer is when you do not really know

guest someone who is invited

guide **1** someone or something that shows people which way to go
2 ***guide dog*** a dog trained to help a blind person

Guide a girl who is a member of the Girl Guides Association

guilt **1** the fact that someone has done something wrong
2 a feeling you have when you know you have done something wrong

guilty full of guilt

guinea pig a furry animal that has no tail and is kept as a pet

guitar a musical instrument with strings across it that you play with your fingers

gulf sea that fills a very large bend in the land

gulp to swallow very quickly
I ***gulped*** *down my tea and rushed out.*

gum **1** the hard pink part of the mouth that holds the teeth
2 a sweet that you chew
3 glue

gunpowder a black powder used for blowing up things

gurgle to make the noise water makes as it goes down the hole in a bath

gush to move like water rushing out of a tap

gust a sudden rush of wind or air

gutter a long, narrow hollow at the side of a street or along the edge of a roof. Gutters take away rain water.

Hh

habit anything that you do without thinking, because you have done it so often

had see **have**

haddock a sea fish that can be eaten

haggard looking ill and very tired
*a **haggard** face*

hail small pieces of ice that fall from the sky like rain

hair a soft covering that grows on the heads and bodies of people and animals

hairdresser someone whose job is to cut people's hair, wash it, or arrange it in a special way

half one of the two equal parts something can be divided into. It can also be written as $\frac{1}{2}$.
*Two **halves** make a whole.*

hall **1** the part inside a house near the front door
2 a very big room
*a school **hall***
3 a large, important building or house
*the Town **Hall***

hallo, hello the word you say when you meet someone

Hallowe'en the 31st October when some people think that magic things happen

halt to stop

halter a rope or strap put round an animal's head or neck so that it can be controlled

halve to divide into two equal parts

halves more than one **half**

hammer a heavy tool used for hitting nails

hammock a bed that is a piece of cloth hung from something by cords joined to each corner

hamper **1** a big basket with a lid
*a picnic **hamper***

2 to make it difficult for someone to do something

hamster a small brown animal that has smooth fur and is kept as a pet

hand the part joined to the lower end of the arm

handcuffs a pair of metal rings used for locking someone's wrists together

handicap anything that makes it more difficult for you to do something

handkerchief a square of material used for blowing the nose

handle **1** a part put on something so that you can get hold of it
2 to touch, feel, hold, or use something with your hands

handsome attractive. Men and boys can be handsome.

hang to fix the top part of something to a hook or nail
I **hung** up my coat and went in.

hangar a shed for keeping an aeroplane in

hanger something used for hanging up things

happen **1** to take place
*This must not **happen** again.*
2 to do something by chance
*I just **happened** to see it.*

happiness the feeling you have when you are very pleased or enjoying yourself

happy full of happiness

harbour a place where boats can stay safely in the water when they are not out at sea

hard **1** not soft
hard ground
2 difficult
hard sums
3 severe
*a **hard** punishment*

hardly only just
hardly able to walk

hare an animal like a big rabbit that can move very quickly

harm to hurt or spoil someone or something

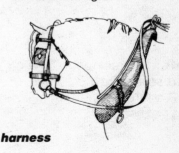

harness

93

harness the set of straps put over a horse's head and round its neck so that it can be controlled
(see **bridle**)

harp a musical instrument.

It has a large frame with strings stretched across it that are played with the fingers.

harsh not kind or gentle
a **harsh** voice

harvest the time when farmers gather in the fruit, corn, or vegetables they have grown

has see **have**

haste hurry

hatch to break out of an egg. Baby birds, insects, fish, and snakes hatch.

hatchet a light tool like an axe for chopping

hate to have a very strong feeling against someone or something you do not like

haughty too proud of yourself

haul to pull with all your strength

haunted often visited by ghosts
a **haunted** house

have   **1** to own
She **has** a new car.
We **haven't** got a car.
2 to contain
It once **had** sweets in it.
It **hasn't** any in it now.
3 to enjoy or suffer
We're **having** a good time.
He's **had** an accident.

hawk a bird that hunts and eats smaller animals

hay dry grass used to feed animals

haze damp or hot air that it is difficult to see through

hazel   **1** a small nut tree
2 the light brown colour of a hazel nut

head   **1** the part of a person or animal that contains the brain, eyes, and mouth
2 the person in charge

headache a pain in the head that goes on hurting

headmaster a man in charge of all the teachers and pupils in a school

headmistress a woman in charge of all the teachers and pupils in a school

heal 1 to make well again
2 to become well again
The cut **healed** *quickly.*

health 1 the state someone's body and mind are in
2 good health

healthy 1 not ill or injured in any way
2 good for people's health
healthy air

heap an untidy pile

hear to take in sounds through the ears
I **heard** *you shout so I came.*

heart 1 the part of the body that makes the blood go round inside
2 the curved shape of a heart. Red hearts are printed on some playing-cards.

hearth the part of the floor where the fire is

heat 1 the hot feeling

that comes from the sun or a fire
2 to make hot

heath wild, flat land with small bushes, but no trees

heather a low bush with small purple, pink, or white flowers. Heather grows on heaths and moors.

heave to lift or pull something heavy

heaven 1 the place where God is thought to live
2 a very happy place

heavy weighing a lot. It is difficult to lift and carry heavy things.

hedge a kind of wall made by bushes growing close together

hedgehog a small animal covered in stiff hairs like sharp needles

heel the back part of the foot

height 1 how high something is
2 a high place

heir (*say* air) someone who will be given money, property, or a title when their owner dies

heiress a girl or woman who will be given money,

property, or a title when their owner dies

helicopter a kind of small aeroplane that can rise straight up into the air. It has large blades that spin round on its roof.

helm the handle or wheel that is used to steer a ship

helmet a strong covering that protects the head
a crash **helmet**

help to do something useful for someone else

helpless not able to look after yourself. Babies are completely helpless.

helter-skelter a tall slide at a fair. You go round and round as you slide down it.

hem the edge of a piece of cloth, that is folded under and sewn down

herb a plant used in cooking to give the food a better flavour

herd a number of cattle that feed together

here in or to this place
Come **here**!

hermit someone who lives alone and keeps away from everyone else

hero a boy or man who has

done something very brave

heroine a girl or woman who has done something very brave

herring a sea fish that can be eaten

herself **1** she and no one else
2 *by herself* on her own

hesitate to wait a little before you do or say something, because you are not sure about it

hibernate to sleep for a long time during the cold weather. Bats, tortoises, and hedgehogs all hibernate.

hiccup to make a sudden, sharp sound. People hiccup when they have eaten or drunk very quickly or laughed a lot.

hide **1** to get into a place where you cannot be seen
I'm **hiding** *over here.*
I **hid** *behind the tree last time.*
2 to put into a secret place
The gold was **hidden** *in a cave.*

hiding-place a place where someone or something is hidden

high **1** going a long way up

a **high** mountain
2 a long way up
It flew **high** into the air.

highwayman a man on a horse, who stopped people on the roads and robbed them. Dick Turpin was a famous highwayman.

hijack to take control of an aeroplane while it is flying and make it go where you want it to go

hill ground that is higher than the ground around it

himself **1** he and no one else
2 **by himself** on his own

hinder to get in someone's way so that it is difficult for him to do something

hinge a metal fastener that joins a door to a wall and lets the door swing backwards and forwards

hint **1** a useful idea
2 to give someone information without telling him exactly what you mean

hip **1** the bony part of the body that sticks out at the side between the waist and thigh
2 a red berry on the wild rose

hippopotamus a very large, heavy, African animal that lives near water. It has tusks and very thick skin.

hire to pay to get the use of something

hiss to make the long sss sound that snakes make

history finding out about things that happened in the past

hive a kind of box for keeping bees in

hoard a secret store of money or other things

hoarse sounding rough and deep. People with sore throats have hoarse voices.

hobble to walk with difficulty because there is something wrong with your leg or foot

hobby something interesting that people like doing in their spare time

hoe a tool for getting rid of weeds

hold **1** to have something in your hands
*I **held** up the picture I had done.*
2 to have room inside for something
3 the place inside a ship where things are kept

hole a gap or opening made in something

holiday time off from school or work

hollow **1** with an empty space inside
*a **hollow** Easter egg*
2 a kind of hole

holly a tree that has shiny, prickly leaves and red berries in the winter

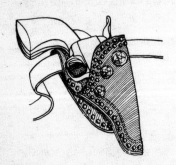

holster a case for putting a gun in. Holsters are worn on straps or belts.

holy special because it belongs to God

home the place where you live

honest not stealing, cheating, or telling lies
*an **honest** man*

honey sweet, sticky food made by bees

honour great respect

hood a covering of soft material for the head and neck

hoof the hard part round a horse's foot

hook a piece of bent metal for hanging things on or catching hold of something

hoop a big wooden or metal ring used in games

hoot to make the sound made by an owl or the horn in a car

hope to want something that you think is likely to happen

hopeless **1** very bad at doing something
2 without hope

hopscotch a game where you hop and throw or kick a stone into squares drawn on the ground

horizon the line where the sky and the land or sea seem to meet

horizontal **1** flat and level

2 *a horizontal line* a straight line across something

horn a kind of pointed bone that grows on the heads of some animals. Bulls and rams have horns.
2 a brass musical instrument that you blow

horrible 1 nasty
a **horrible** sight
2 frightening
a **horrible** film

horrid nasty
a **horrid** dream

horror very great fear

horse an animal with hooves that is used for riding and pulling carts

horse-chestnut the big tree that conkers grow on

horseshoe a flat piece of metal fixed underneath a horse's hoof and shaped like this Ω

hose-pipe a long plastic or rubber tube that water can go through

hospital a place where people who are ill or hurt are looked after

hotel a building where people pay to have meals and stay for the night

hound a dog used for hunting

hour sixty minutes

house a building where people live together

household all the people who live together in the same house

hover 1 to stay in one place in the air
2 to wait near someone or something and have nothing to do

hovercraft a machine that is like both an aeroplane and a boat. It travels quickly just above the surface of land or water.

how in what way
How did you know?

howl to give a long, loud cry like an animal in pain

hub the part at the centre of a

wheel, where the spokes meet

huddle to keep close to others in a group because you are cold or frightened

huge very big

hull the main part of a boat or ship

hum **1** to sing a tune with your lips close
2 to make the sound a bee makes

human any man, woman, or child

humble not proud
a *humble* person

humorous amusing

hump one of the big lumps on a camel's back

hung see **hang**

hunger the need for food

hungry feeling hunger

hunt **1** to go after a wild animal because you want to kill it
2 to look carefully for something

hurl to throw something as far as you can

hurrah, hurray a word that you shout when you are very glad about something

hurricane a storm with a very strong wind

hurry **1** to move quickly
2 to try to do something quickly because there is not enough time

hurt to make a person or animal feel pain
I ***hurt*** *my knee when I fell down.*

hurtle to move very quickly

husband a man married to someone

hustle **1** to hurry
2 to push someone roughly

hutch a kind of box for keeping a rabbit in

hyacinth a flower that grows from a bulb and has a very sweet smell

hymn a song that praises God

hyphen a mark like this - used in writing to join parts of words together

ice **1** water that has frozen hard

2 to put icing on cakes

iceberg a large piece of ice floating in the sea

ice cream a sweet frozen food that tastes of cream

icicle a thin, pointed piece of ice hanging down

icing a sweet, sticky mixture spread over the tops of cakes to decorate them. Some icing goes very hard when it is dry.

idea **1** something you have thought of yourself
2 a plan

ideal just what you want

identical exactly the same
identical twins

idiot a very stupid person

idle doing nothing
idle hands

idol something people worship and treat as if it were God

igloo a round house made of blocks of hard snow

ignition-key the key used to start the engine of a car

ignorant knowing nothing or only a little
an ignorant fool

ignore to take no notice of someone

ill not well

illness something that makes people ill. Measles, chicken-pox, and colds are illnesses.

ill-treat to treat badly

illuminations a lot of bright, coloured lights used to decorate streets, buildings, or parks

illustration a picture in a book

101

imaginary not real

imagination the ability to make pictures in your mind of things and people you cannot see

imagine to make a picture in your mind of someone or something you cannot see

imitate to copy a person or animal

imitation a copy that is not as valuable as the real thing
imitation cream

immediately straight away

immense very big

impatient not patient

impertinent rude
an *impertinent* child

implore to beg someone to do something for you

important **1** powerful and worth respect
a very *important* person
2 worth looking at or thinking about seriously
an *important* notice

impossible not possible

impress to make people think you are very good at something

impression an idea you have that may be wrong

impressive so wonderful that you will always remember it

imprison to put someone in prison

improve **1** to become better **2** to make something better

incense something that gives a sweet smell when it is burnt

inch a measure for length

include to make something part of a group of other things

incorrect not correct

increase **1** to make bigger **2** to become bigger

indeed really
very wet **indeed**

index a list at the back of a book. It tells you what things are in the book and where to find them.

indignant angry because something unfair has been done or said

indoors inside a building

industry **1** hard work **2** work done in factories

infant a young child

infectious likely to spread to others
an *infectious* illness

inform to tell someone something

information words that tell people about something

infuriate to make very angry

ingenious clever at thinking of new ways of doing or making things

inhabit to live in a place

initial (*say* in-ish-ul) the first letter of a name *William Brown's **initials** are W.B.*

injection a prick in the skin made by a hollow needle filled with medicine so that the medicine goes into the body. Injections can make people better or stop them getting illnesses.

injure to harm

injury harm done to part of the body

ink a coloured liquid used for writing with a pen

inland in a part of the country that is not near the sea

inn a kind of small hotel

innings a turn at batting in cricket

innocent not guilty

inquiry **1** a question

2 a search to find out all about something

inquisitive full of a wish to know about something. Inquisitive people often want to know about things that they have no right to know about.

insect a tiny creature with six legs. Flies, ants, butterflies, and bees are all insects.

inside **1** in something
2 the part nearest the middle

insist to be very firm in saying or doing something
*He **insists** on staying up late.*

insolent very rude
***insolent** behaviour*

inspect to look carefully at people or things

inspector **1** an important policeman
2 someone whose job is to check that things are done properly

instalment **1** a part of a story that is told in parts
2 an amount of money people pay every week or every month in order to buy something

instantly at once

instead in place of something else

instinct something that makes animals do things they have not learnt to do. *Spiders spin webs by* **instinct**.

instruction words that tell people what to do

instructor a kind of teacher

instrument **1** a tool or something else used for doing a job
2 something used for making musical sounds

insult to hurt someone's feelings by being rude

intelligent able to learn and understand things easily

intend to mean to do something

intense very great
intense heat

interest to make someone want to find out more, look, or listen

interfere **1** to get in the way
2 to take part in something that has nothing to do with you

international belonging to more than one country
an **international** competition

interrupt to stop someone from carrying on with what he is saying or doing

interval the time between parts of a play or film

interview to ask someone questions to find out what he thinks about something or what he is like

introduce to make someone known to other people

invade to go into another country to fight against the people there

invalid someone who is weak because he is ill or injured

invent to be the first person to think of a plan for a new machine or a better way of doing something

investigate to try to find out as much as you can about something

invisible not able to be seen
invisible ink

invitation words that ask you politely to come
a party **invitation**

invite to ask someone politely to come or do something

iris **1** the coloured part of the eye
2 a plant with leaves shaped like swords and yellow,

white, blue, or purple flowers

iron **1** a strong, heavy metal
2 a flat piece of metal with a handle. It is heated and used for making clothes smooth and flat.

ironmonger someone who keeps a shop that sells tools, nails, and other metal things

irritable easily annoyed

irritate to keep annoying someone

island, isle a piece of land with water all around it

italic **1** a kind of writing
2 a kind of printing *like this*

itch a feeling in your skin that makes you want to scratch yourself

item any one thing in a list or group of things

itself **1** it and nothing else
2 *by itself* on its own

ivory **1** something that comes from the tusks of elephants. It is pale cream, hard, and very valuable.
2 the pale cream colour of ivory

ivy a climbing plant with shiny dark green leaves

Jj

jab **1** to push roughly at something with your finger or the end of a stick
2 to hit something suddenly with the pointed part of a sharp tool

jackdaw a black bird. Jackdaws sometimes steal bright things and hide them.

jacket a kind of short coat

jagged with sharp parts along the edge

jam **1** fruit boiled with sugar until it is thick
raspberry **jam**
2 a lot of people or cars crowded together so that it is difficult to move
a traffic **jam**
3 to become fixed and difficult to move
The door has **jammed** and I can't open it.

jar a container like the glass ones used for jam

jaw **1** the lower part of the face
2 one of the bones that hold the teeth

jealous unhappy because someone else seems to have

more or be doing better than you

jeans strong cotton trousers

jeep a very strong small car

jeer to make fun of someone because you think you are better than he is

jelly a sweet, shiny, slippery food that looks solid, though it melts in your mouth
*orange **jelly***

jerk to move suddenly or clumsily

jersey something with sleeves that is knitted and worn on the top half of the body

jet **1** a liquid or gas coming very quickly out of a small opening
2 an aeroplane with an engine that is driven by jets of hot gas

jewel a valuable and beautiful stone

jewellery necklaces, bracelets, rings, and brooches

jigsaw puzzle a set of small pieces of cardboard or wood that fit together to make a picture

jingle to make the sound tiny bells make

jockey someone who rides horses in races

jog **1** to run slowly
2 to push against something

join **1** to put together to make one thing
2 to become a member of a group

joiner someone whose job is to make furniture and other things out of wood

joint **1** the place where two parts fit together. The ankle is the joint between the foot and the leg.
2 a large piece of meat

joke something said or done to make people laugh

jolly happy and gay

jolt to shake suddenly

jotter a book where you can write things down quickly

journey the travelling people do to get from one place to another place

joy great happiness

judge 1 to decide whether something is good or bad, right or wrong, fair or unfair
2 someone who judges

juggler someone who entertains people by doing difficult throwing, catching, and balancing tricks

juice the liquid in fruit and vegetables

jumble a lot of different things all mixed up

jump to move up suddenly from the ground into the air

jumper a jersey

junction a place where roads or railway lines meet

jungle a forest in a very hot, damp country

junior younger

junk things that people do not want any more

just 1 fair
a **just** king
2 exactly
It's **just** what I wanted.
3 only
Just one more cake, please.

Kk

kaleidoscope a thick tube you look through to see coloured patterns. The pattern changes when you turn the end of the tube.

kangaroo an Australian animal that jumps. Female kangaroos have pouches in which they carry their babies.

keel the long piece of wood or metal along the bottom of a boat

keen 1 very interested in something
2 sharp
a **keen** knife

keep 1 to have something as your own and not get rid of it. He **kept** the money he found.

2 to make something stay as it is

3 to look after something

kennel a little hut for keeping a dog in

kept see **keep**

kerb the blocks of stone along the edge of the pavement

kernel the part in the middle of a nut

kettle a metal container in which water is boiled. It has a lid, handle, and spout.

key **1** a piece of metal shaped so that it fits into a lock
2 a small lever pressed with the finger. Pianos and typewriters have keys.

kick to hit something with your foot

kid a very young goat

kidnap to take someone away and keep him prisoner until you get what you want

kill to make someone or something die

kilogramme a measure for weight
a **kilogramme** of apples

kilometre (say <u>kil</u>-o-meeter or kil-<u>om</u>-it-er)
a measure for length
1 **kilometre**=1,000 metres

kilt a kind of pleated skirt worn by some Scotsmen

kind **1** ready to help and love other people
2 a sort
a special **kind** of paint

king a man who has been crowned as ruler of a country

kingdom a land that is ruled by a king or queen

kingfisher a brightly coloured bird that lives near water and catches fish

kiosk **1** a telephone box

2 a small stall that sells newspapers, sweets, and tobacco

kipper a dried fish that is ready to be cooked and eaten. Kippers have a strong taste.

kiss to touch someone with your lips because you are fond of him or her

kitchen the room where food is cooked

kite a light frame covered in cloth or paper and flown in the wind at the end of a long piece of string

kitten a very young cat

knee the bony part in the middle of the leg where it bends

kneel to get down on your knees
They **knelt** down and prayed.

knew see **know**

knickers a piece of underwear worn by women and girls

knife a tool with a long, sharp edge for cutting things
two **knives**

knight **1** a man who has been given the title, Sir

Sir Francis Drake was a **knight**.
2 a man in armour who rode into battle on a horse

knit to use wool and a pair of long needles to make clothes

knives more than one **knife**

knob the round handle on a door or drawer

knock **1** to hit something hard
2 to hit something by accident

knot the twisted part where pieces of string, rope, cotton, or ribbon have been tied together

know **1** to have something in your mind that you have found out
I **knew** all about it yesterday.
2 to have met someone before
I haven't **known** her long.

knowledge things that are known and understood

known see **know**

knuckle one of the places where the fingers bend

koala bear a furry Australian animal that looks like a small bear

Ll

label a piece of card or sticky paper put on something to show what it is, whose it is, or where it is going

laboratory a room or building where scientific work is done

labour hard work

Labrador a kind of large black or light brown dog

lace **1** thin, pretty material with a pattern of holes in it. Lace is often used to decorate things.
2 a piece of thin cord used to tie up a shoe

lack to be without something

ladder two long bars with short bars between them that you can climb up or down

ladle a big, deep spoon used for serving soup

lady **1** a polite name for a woman
2 a title
Lady Jane Grey

ladybird a red or yellow insect with black spots on it that can fly

lag to be behind because you are moving too slowly
He's *lagging* behind again.

laid see **lay**

lain see **lie**

lair a wild animal's home

lake a large area of water with land all around it

lamb a young sheep

lame not able to walk properly

lamp something that gives light where you want it

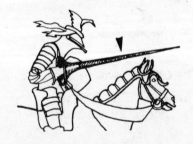

lance a long spear like the ones used by knights long ago

land **1** all the dry parts of the earth's surface

2 a country
3 to arrive by boat or aeroplane

landing the flat place at the top of the stairs in a building

landlady a woman who lets other people live in her house or flat in return for money

landlord a man who lets other people live in his house or flat in return for money

lane a narrow road

language words spoken or written by people
foreign **languages**

lantern a container for a light. It is made of metal and glass or something else that the light can shine through.

lap **1** the part from the waist to the knees of a person sitting down
2 once round a race course

3 to drink with the tongue, like a cat

larch a kind of tree. Larches have small cones and lose their leaves every winter.

lard white fat from pigs, used in cooking

larder a cool cupboard or small room where food is kept

large big

lark a small, brown bird that sings

lash **1** to tie tightly to something
2 to hit hard, usually with a whip

lasso (*say* las-soo)
a long rope with a loop at the end, tied so that the loop can get bigger or smaller. Cowboys use lassos for catching cattle.

last **1** after all the others
2 to go on for some time

latch a fastener on a gate or door

late **1** after the expected time
2 near the end of a day, month, or year
3 no longer alive
the **late** *King*

lather soap bubbles on the top of water

laugh to make sounds that show that you are happy or think something is very funny

laughter the sound of laughing

launch (*say* lornch)
1 a large boat with an engine
2 to push a boat into the water
3 to send a space ship from earth into space

launderette a place with washing-machines that people can pay to use

laundry (*say* lorndree)
1 clothes that need to be washed
2 a place where people send dirty clothes and sheets to be washed

lavatory a place where the body can get rid of its waste

lavender **1** a bush with pale purple flowers that smell very sweet
2 a pale purple colour

law a rule or set of rules that everyone in a country must keep

lawn the part of a garden that is covered with short grass

lay **1** to put something down
2 *to lay the table* to get the table ready for a meal
3 to make an egg
The hen laid two eggs today.
4 see **lie**

layer something flat that lies over or under another surface

lazy not willing to work

lead¹ (*rhymes with* bed)
a soft, grey metal that is very heavy

lead² (*rhymes with* seed)
1 to go in front of other people to show them where to go or what to do
He found us and led us to safety.
2 to be in charge of a group
3 a strap fastened to a dog's collar so that you can control him

leader a person or animal that leads

leaf one of the flat green parts that grow on trees and other plants

league a group of teams that play matches against each other

leak to have a hole or crack that liquid or gas can get through
This kettle leaks.

lean **1** to bend your body

towards something
*I **leant** forward and looked.*
2 to rest against something
3 to make something slope
4 not fat
lean meat

leant (*say* lent)
see **lean**

leap to jump
*I **leapt** up as if I'd been stung.*

leapt (*say* lept)
see **leap**

leap year a year with an extra day in it, the 29th February. A leap year comes once every four years.

learn **1** to find out about something
2 to find out how to do something
*He **learnt** to read last year.*

leash a dog's lead

least **1** less than all the others
*the **least** expensive bike*
2 the smallest amount

leather a strong material made from the skins of animals
leather shoes

leave **1** to go from a person or place
2 to let something stay

where it is
*I've **left** my book at home.*

leaves more than one **leaf**

led see **lead²**

ledge a narrow shelf like the one that sticks out under a window

leek a long, white vegetable with green leaves that tastes like an onion

left **1** on the side opposite the right. Most people hold a fork in their left hand and a knife in their right hand.
2 see **leave**

left-handed using the left hand to write and do other important things, because you find it easier than using the right hand

legend a story that was first told long ago by people who thought it was true. Most legends are not true.

leisure (*rhymes with* treasure) time when you can do what you want to do, because you do not have to work

lemon **1** a pale yellow fruit with a sour taste
2 the pale yellow colour of lemons

lemonade a drink made from lemons, sugar, and water

lend to let someone have something of yours for a short time
I **lent** *you my bike yesterday.*

length **1** how long something is
2 a piece of rope or cloth

lengthen **1** to make longer
2 to get longer

lens a curved piece of glass or plastic that makes light go where it is needed. Spectacles, cameras, and telescopes have lenses.

lent see **lend**

leopard a big wild cat found in Africa and Asia. It has yellow fur with black spots on it.

leotard (*say* lee-a-tard) a piece of clothing worn by acrobats and dancers

leotard

less **1** not as much
2 take away. Six less four is two, $6-4=2$.

lessen **1** to make less
2 to become less

lesson **1** the time when someone is teaching you
2 something that you have to learn

letter **1** one of the signs used for writing words, such as a, b, or c
2 a written message sent to another person

lettuce a vegetable with green leaves that are eaten in salads

level **1** flat and smooth
level ground
2 equal
Your scores are **level***.*

lever a bar that is pulled down to lift something heavy or make a machine work

liar someone who tells lies

library a building or room where a lot of books are kept for people to use

licence a printed paper that says that you can do, own, or use something
a dog licence

lick to move the tongue over something

lie **1** to rest with the body flat as it is in bed
I lay down and went to sleep.
The cat has lain here all night.
He has been lying here.
2 to say something that is not true
You lied to me yesterday.
He was lying.
3 something you say that is not true
He tells lies.

life the time between birth and death
Do cats have nine lives?

lifeboat a boat that goes out to sea in bad weather to save people's lives

lift **1** to move upwards
2 to pick up something
3 a machine for taking people or things up and down inside a building

4 a ride in someone's car or lorry

light **1** the power that makes things able to be seen. Light comes from the sun, the stars, flames, and lamps.
2 to start something burning
I struck a match and lit the fire.
3 pale
light blue
4 weighing little
as light as a feather

lighten **1** to make lighter
2 to get lighter

lighthouse a tower with a bright light that warns ships of rocks or other dangers

lightning the bright light that flashes in the sky during a thunderstorm

like **1** to think someone or something is pleasant
2 nearly the same as another person or thing

likely expected to happen or to be true

lilac **1** a tree with a lot of white or pale purple flowers that smell very sweet
2 a pale purple colour

lily a beautiful white flower grown in gardens

limb a leg, arm, or wing

lime **1** a white powder used in making cement
2 a pale green fruit like a lemon
3 a kind of tree

limit a line or point that people cannot or should not pass
*a speed **limit***

limp **1** to walk with difficulty because there is something wrong with your leg or foot
2 not stiff

line **1** a long, thin mark like this

2 a row of people or things
3 the set of metal rails a train moves along

linen strong cloth used for making sheets and table-cloths

liner a big ship for taking people on long journeys

linger to be slow to leave

lining cloth covering the inside of clothes or curtains

link **1** to join things together
2 one of the rings in a chain

lino, linoleum a stiff, shiny covering for the floor

lint soft material for putting on an injured part of the body

lion a large, light brown wild cat found in Africa and India

lioness a female lion

lipstick something that looks like a crayon and is used for colouring lips

liquid anything that is like water, oil, or milk

liquorice a black sweet that you get in sticks and other shapes

list a group of things or names written down one after the other
*a shopping **list***

listen to pay attention in order to hear something

lit see **light**

litre (*rhymes with* Peter) a measure for liquid
*a **litre** of paint*

litter **1** paper, empty packets, bottles, and other rubbish, dropped or left lying about
2 all the young animals born to the same mother at the same time

little **1** not big
*a **little** boy*
2 not much
***little** time*

live[1] (*rhymes with* give)
1 to have your life
2 to have your home in a place

live² (*rhymes with* dive)
alive

lively full of life and energy
*a **lively** dance, a **lively***
horse

lives (*rhymes with* dives)
more than one **life**

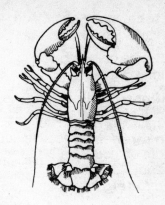

lobster

lizard a creature with skin like
a snake and four legs

load **1** something that is
carried
2 to put things on to
something that will carry
them
3 to put bullets into a gun

loaf bread in the shape it was
baked in
*two **loaves***

loan anything that is lent to
someone

loaves more than one **loaf**

lobster a sea creature with a
shell, two large claws, eight
legs, and a tail

local belonging to one place
local radio

loch a lake in Scotland

lock **1** to fasten with a key
2 a fastening for a door,
gate, or box that is opened
with a key
3 a piece of hair

locomotive the engine that
pulls a train

locust an insect that flies
about in a large group,
destroying plants by eating
them

lodge **1** to pay to live in
someone else's house
2 a small house near the
gates of a large garden that
belongs to a much bigger
house

lodger someone who pays to
live in another person's
home

loft a room in the roof, where
things can be kept

loiter to stand about with nothing to do

loll to sit or lie in an untidy, lazy way

lollipop a big sweet on the end of a stick

lonely **1** sad because you are on your own
2 far from others
a **lonely** house

long **1** measuring a lot from one end to the other
a **long** road
2 taking a lot of time
a **long** holiday
3 **to long for** to want something very much

look **1** to use your eyes
2 **to look for** to try to find something
3 to seem
You **look** sad.

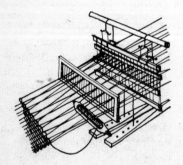

loom a machine for weaving cloth

loop a ring made in rope, wire, thread, or ribbon

loose (*say* looss)
1 not tight
2 not fixed to anything

loosen **1** to make looser
2 to get looser

loot things that have been stolen

lord **1** a nobleman
2 a title
Lord Baden-Powell

lorry a big, open truck for taking heavy things by road to different places

lose (*say* looz)
1 to be without something you once had
2 to be without something, because you cannot find it
I've **lost** my coat.
3 to be beaten in a game
We **lost** last Saturday's match.

lost see **lose**

lotion a liquid that is put on the skin

loud **1** very easy to hear
2 noisy

loudspeaker **1** a machine that makes sound louder
2 the part of a television, radio or record-player that the sound comes from

loudspeaker

lounge a room with comfortable chairs in it

love to like very much

lovely **1** beautiful
*a **lovely** face*
2 pleasing
*a **lovely** idea*

low not high

loyal always true to your friends

luck the way things happen that have not been planned

lucky having good luck
*a **lucky** charm*

luggage bags, boxes, and suitcases taken by someone on a journey

lukewarm only just warm

lullaby a song that is sung to send a baby to sleep

lumber **1** rough wood
2 old furniture and other things that are no longer used
3 to move in a clumsy way

lump **1** a solid piece with no clear shape
*a **lump** of clay*
2 a swelling

lunch a meal eaten in the middle of the day

lung one of the two parts inside the body used for breathing

lurch to lean suddenly to one side

lurk to wait where you cannot be seen

luxury something expensive that you like very much but do not really need

lying see **lie**

Mm

mac short for **mackintosh**

machine something with several parts that work together to do a job
*a washing-**machine***

machine-gun a gun that can

119

keep firing very quickly for a long time

machinery machines

mackintosh a raincoat

madam a word sometimes used when speaking politely to a woman, instead of her name

made see **make**

magazine a kind of thin book that comes out every week or month with different stories and pictures in it

maggot a tiny worm that comes from an egg laid by a fly

magic the power to do wonderful things or clever tricks that people cannot usually do

magician someone who knows a lot about magic and uses it

magnet a metal bar that can make pieces of iron or steel come and stick to it

magnificent **1** very grand
a **magnificent** palace
2 splendid
a **magnificent** present

magnify to make something look bigger
a **magnifying** glass

magpie a black and white bird. Magpies sometimes steal bright things and hide them.

maid a girl or woman who is a servant

mail letters, cards, and parcels sent through the post

main the most important
a **main** road

majesty a word used when speaking to a king or queen
Your **Majesty**

make **1** to get something new by putting other things together
I've **made** a boat out of paper and wood.
2 to cause something to happen
You **made** me do this last time.

make-up cream, lipstick, and powder put on the face to make it look different

male any person or animal that can become a father.

Men, boys, stags, and bulls are all males.

mammal any animal that has hair and can feed its babies with its own milk

man a fully grown male
two **men**

manage **1** to be in charge of a shop or factory
2 to be able to do something although it is difficult

mane the long hair along a horse's back or on a lion's head and neck

manger a long, narrow container that horses and cattle can eat from when they are in the stable

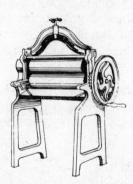

mangle **1** a machine for pressing water out of wet clothes
2 to cut up or crush something badly

manner the way something happens or is done

manners your behaviour towards other people

manor a big, important house in the country

mansion a big, important house

mantelpiece the shelf above a fire-place

manufacture to make large numbers of the same thing

many a large number of people or things

map a diagram that shows part of the world and where different places are

marble **1** a small, glass ball used in some games
2 a kind of smooth stone used for building or making statues

march to walk like soldiers on parade

mare a female horse

margarine a food that looks and tastes like butter, but is not made from milk

margin the empty space between the edge of a page and the writing or pictures

marigold a bright orange or

yellow flower grown in gardens

mark **1** a stain, spot, or line that spoils something
dirty **marks**
2 a sign or number put on a piece of work to show how good or bad it is

market a group of stalls selling food and other things. Markets are usually held in the open air.

marmalade jam made from oranges or lemons

maroon **1** a very dark red colour
2 to leave someone in a wild and lonely place without any way of escaping from it

marriage a wedding

marry to become someone's husband or wife

marsh a piece of very wet ground

marvellous wonderful
a **marvellous** *story*

marzipan a sweet food made from almonds

mash to crush something to make it soft and get rid of the lumps
mashed *potato*

mask a covering worn on the face to protect or hide it

mass a large number or amount
masses *of flowers*

massive very big

mast a tall pole that holds up a ship's sails, a flag, or an aerial

master a man who is in charge

match **1** a small, thin stick that gives a flame when rubbed on something rough
2 a game played between two sides
3 to be the same as another thing or like it in some way

material **1** anything used for making something else
2 wool, cotton, or anything else that is woven and used for making clothes or covers

mathematics, maths finding out about numbers, measurement, and shapes

matter **1** to be important
2 something you need to think about or do
a serious **matter**
3 **What's the matter?** What is wrong?

mattress the thick, soft part of a bed

may 1 can
May I go out to play?
2 will perhaps
*It **may** rain later.*
*It **might** rain later.*

mayor the person in charge of the council in a town or city

maze a set of lines or paths that twist and turn so much that it is very easy to lose the way

meadow a field covered with grass

meal the food eaten at breakfast, lunch, dinner, tea, or supper

mean 1 not generous
2 to plan in your mind
*I **meant** to tell him, but I forgot.*
3 to have a meaning

meaning what someone wants to say with the words he is using

meant (*rhymes with* tent)
see **mean**

meanwhile during the time something else is happening

measles an illness that makes red spots come on the skin

measure 1 to find out how big something is
2 a unit used for measuring.

Kilogrammes, grammes, pounds, and ounces are all measures for weight.

measurement how much something measures

meat the flesh of animals used as food

mechanical worked by or like machinery
*a **mechanical** digger*

medal a piece of metal in the shape of a coin, star, or cross given to someone very brave or very good at something
*a gold **medal***

medallist someone who has won a medal

meddle to take part in something that has nothing to do with you

medicine liquid or tablets that a sick person has to swallow in order to get better again

medium of middle size

meek gentle and not proud

meet 1 to come together
2 to come face to face with another person
*I **met** her in town yesterday.*

meeting a group of people who have come together to

talk about something or to
listen to someone

melon a large, juicy fruit with
a yellow or green skin

melt to change into a liquid
when heated. Ice melts.

member someone who
belongs to a group

memory 1 the ability to
remember
2 anything that is
remembered

men more than one **man**

menagerie (*say* min-aj-er-
ree)
a kind of small zoo

mend to make a damaged
thing as useful as it was
before

mention to speak of something or someone when you
are talking about other things

menu a list of the different
kinds of food you can choose
for your meal

mercy being kind to someone
instead of punishing him
Show **mercy** to the
prisoners.

meringue (*say* mer-rang)
a crisp cake made from the
whites of eggs mixed with
sugar and baked

mermaid a creature in
stories, that looks like a
woman but has a fish's tail
instead of legs

merry happy and gay

mess things that are untidy,
dirty, or mixed up

message words that you
send to someone to tell him
something when you cannot
speak to him yourself

messenger someone who
takes a message to
someone else

met see **meet**

metal something hard that
melts when it is very hot.
Gold, silver, iron, and tin are
all kinds of metal.

meteor a small piece of
rock or metal that moves
through space and burns
up when it gets near the
earth

meteorite a lump of rock or metal that has fallen through space and landed on the earth

meter a machine that measures how much of something has been used *gas* **meters**

method the way you choose to do something

metre a measure for length *1,000* **metres** = *1 kilometre*

mew, miaow (*say* mee-<u>ow</u>) to make the cry a cat makes

mice more than one **mouse**

microphone a machine that changes sound into electricity so that it can be sent along wires to loudspeakers, telephones, or aerials

microscope an instrument that makes it possible to see very tiny things by making them look much bigger

midday twelve o'clock in the day

middle the part of something that is the same distance from all its sides or edges or from both its ends

midget someone who is unusually small

midnight twelve o'clock at night

might see **may**

mild gentle

mile a measure for length

milk a white liquid that mothers and some female animals feed their babies with. People can drink the milk that comes from cows.

mill **1** a place with machinery for making corn into flour **2** a kind of factory

millionaire someone who owns a million pounds

mime to tell someone something by using actions not words

mimic to copy someone's voice in order to make fun of him

mince meat cut into very small pieces

mincemeat a sweet mixture of chopped fruit and other things, cooked inside pastry at Christmas

mind **1** the power to think, feel, and understand
2 to look after
*I'll **mind** the baby.*
3 ***Mind Out**!* Be careful!
4 to be worried or upset by something
*Do you **mind** missing the party?*

mine **1** a place where men work to dig coal, metal, jewels, or salt out of the ground
2 a bomb hidden in the ground or the sea to blow up things that come close to it
3 belonging to me
*That's **mine**.*

miner someone who works down a mine

mineral **1** any useful or valuable rock that people get out of the ground
2 a cold drink with a lot of tiny bubbles in it

mingle to mix

miniature tiny, but just like something much bigger

minister **1** someone who serves God by being in charge of a church

2 an important person in the government

minnow a tiny fish found in rivers, streams, lakes, and ponds

minstrel a man who sang or played music to entertain people long ago

mint **1** a green plant used in cooking to give food a better flavour
2 a sweet that tastes of mint
3 a place where coins are made

minus take away. Six minus two is four, $6 - 2 = 4$.

minute[1] (*say* <u>min</u>-it) sixty seconds

minute[2] (*say* my-<u>newt</u>) very tiny

miracle something wonderful that has happened, although it did not seem possible

mirage (*say* mi-rarj) a trick of the light that makes people see things that are not really there, such as pools of water in deserts

mirror a piece of glass in which you can see yourself

misbehave to be naughty

mischief silly or bad

behaviour that gets you into trouble

mischievous likely to do silly or naughty things

miser someone who has a lot of money, but tries to spend as little as possible so that he can keep it

miserable very unhappy

misery suffering
*great **misery***

misfortune something unlucky that happens

miss 1 to fail to hit, catch, see, hear, or find something
2 to be sad because someone is no longer with you

mission an important job that someone is sent away to do

mist damp air that it is difficult to see through

mistake something you have done or thought that is wrong
*spelling **mistakes***

mistletoe a plant with green leaves and white berries in the winter. It is used to decorate houses at Christmas.

misunderstand to get the wrong idea about something
*You **misunderstood** what I said.*

mitten a kind of glove with two parts, one for the thumb and one for all the fingers

mix to stir or shake different things together to make one thing

mixture something made of different things mixed together

moan 1 to make a soft sound that shows you are in pain or trouble
2 to grumble

moat a ditch dug round a castle and usually filled with water

mock 1 to make fun of someone
2 not real
*a **mock** battle*

model 1 a small copy of something
2 someone whose job is to wear new clothes to show people what they look like

modern of the kind that is usual now
*a **modern** house*

moist damp

mole a small, grey, furry animal that digs holes under the ground

moment a very small amount of time

monarch a ruler who is a king, queen, emperor, or empress

monastery a house where monks live and work

money the coins and pieces of paper people give when they buy things and get when they sell things

mongrel a dog that is a mixture of different kinds of dog

monitor a boy or girl with a special job to do at school

monk one of a group of men who live together and obey rules because of the religion they believe in

monkey an animal with hands, feet it can use like hands, long arms, and a tail

monster 1 a large, frightening animal in stories
2 unusually large

a **monster** *ice cream*

month a measure for time. There are twelve months in a year.

monument a statue or building made so that people will remember someone or something

mood the way you feel
in a good **mood**

moon the planet that goes round the earth and shines in the sky at night. Sometimes it looks completely round and sometimes like part of a circle.

moor 1 an area of land that has bushes but no trees, because it is too windy
2 to tie up a boat so that it will not float away

more 1 a larger number or amount
2 again
I'll tell you once **more**.

morning the time from the beginning of the day until the middle of the day

mortar a mixture of sand, cement, and water, used in building to stick bricks together

mosaic a picture made from coloured pieces of paper,

glass, stone, or wood

moss a plant that grows in damp places and has no flower

most **1** more than any other
2 very
She was **most** kind.

moth an insect with large, coloured wings. Moths usually fly around at night.

mother a female parent

motor the part inside a car or machine that makes it move

motorbike a kind of bicycle with an engine

mould (rhymes with old)
1 furry stuff that sometimes grows on food that has gone bad
2 a container for making things like jelly or plaster set in the shape that is wanted

mound a pile of earth

mount to get on to a horse or bicycle so that you can ride it

mountain a very high hill

mouse a very small animal with a long tail and a pointed nose
three blind **mice**

moustache hair that grows above a man's top lip

mouth the part of the face that opens for eating and speaking

move **1** to take from one place to another
2 to go from one place to another

movement moving
a sudden **movement**

mow to cut grass

much a lot of something

mud wet soil

muddle to mix things up and make a mess of something

mule an animal that is half horse and half donkey

multiply to make something a number of times bigger. Two multiplied by four is eight, $2 \times 4 = 8$.

mumble to speak in a way that is not clear so that it is difficult to hear your words

mumps an illness that makes the sides of the face swell

munch to chew noisily

murder to kill someone on purpose

murmur to speak in a very soft, low voice

muscle one of the parts inside the body that become tight or

loose in order to make the body move

museum a place where a lot of interesting things are kept for people to go and see

mushroom a kind of fungus that people can eat

music the sounds made by someone singing or playing a musical instrument

musical **1** having to do with music
musical instruments
2 good at music

mussel a small sea creature that lives inside a pair of black shells

must have to
I **must** go now.

mustard **1** a yellow powder or liquid used to give food a strong flavour
2 *mustard and cress*

small green plants eaten in salads

mutiny an attack made by soldiers or sailors against the officers in charge of them

mutter to murmur or grumble

mutton meat from a sheep

muzzle **1** an animal's nose and mouth
2 a cover put over an animal's nose and mouth so that it cannot bite

myself **1** I and no one else
2 *by myself* on my own

mysterious strange and puzzling

mystery something strange and puzzling that has happened

Nn

nag to keep telling someone that you are not pleased and that he ought to behave differently

nail **1** the hard part that covers the end of each finger and toe
2 a small piece of metal with a sharp point, used for

fastening pieces of wood together

naked (*say* nake-id) without any clothes or covering

name what you call someone or something

nanny-goat a female goat

nappy a piece of cloth put round a baby's bottom

narrow not wide

nasty **1** not pleasant
a **nasty** day
2 very dirty
a **nasty** mess
3 not kind
a **nasty** person

nation a country and the people who live in it

national belonging to one country

native someone born in the place that you are thinking of
a **native** of Scotland

natural **1** made by nature, not by people or machines
2 normal
It is **natural** for birds to fly.

nature **1** plants, animals, the sea, and everything else in the world that was not made by people

2 what a person or animal is really like

naughty badly behaved

navigate to make sure that a ship, aeroplane, or car is going in the right direction

navy **1** a group of ships and the people trained to use them for fighting
2 dark blue

near not far away

nearly not quite
nearly 3 o'clock, **nearly** £100
nearly there

neat tidy

necessary needed very much

neck the part of the body that joins the head to the shoulders

necklace beads, jewels, or a chain worn round the neck

nectar a sweet liquid inside flowers. Bees collect nectar to make honey.

need **1** to be without something that you ought to have
2 to have to do something
I **need** to go to the dentist.

needle **1** a very thin, pointed piece of metal. Needles used for sewing have holes in them.

2 one of a pair of rods used for knitting

3 a very thin, pointed leaf. Pine trees have needles.

neglect to leave something alone and not look after it

Negro someone with a black skin
two **Negroes**

neigh to make the noise a horse makes

neighbour someone who lives next door or near to you

neither not either
Neither *of the twins has a bike.*

nephew the son of a brother or sister

nerve **1** one of the small parts inside the body that carry messages to and from the brain, so that the body can feel and move
2 brave or calm behaviour when there is danger
Don't lose your **nerve**.

nervous **1** afraid and excited because of something you have to do
2 easily frightened
a **nervous** *animal*

nest a cosy place made by birds, mice, and some other animals for their babies

nestle to curl up comfortably

netball a ball game played outside between two teams of girls. The ball has to be thrown into a net on a tall post.

nettle a plant with its stem and leaves covered in hairs that sting

never not ever

new **1** just bought or made
a **new** *bike*
2 different
my **new** *school*

news words that tell you about something that has just happened

newspaper large sheets of paper folded together, with the news printed on them. Most newspapers come out every day.

newt a small creature that lives near water and has four legs and a long tail

next the nearest

nib the pointed metal part at the end of the kind of pen that needs ink

nibble to eat something by biting off a little at a time. Rabbits nibble carrots.

nice pleasant

nickname a name you call someone instead of his real name. William Cody's nickname was Buffalo Bill.

niece the daughter of a brother or sister

night the time when it is dark

nightingale a small, brown bird that sings at night

nightmare a frightening dream

nimble able to move quickly and easily

nip to bite someone or squeeze his skin between the thumb and finger

nitwit someone who is very silly

noble brave and generous

nobleman a man who is a duke or lord

nobody no person

noise sound that is loud and often not pleasant

none not any or not one

nonsense something that does not mean anything

noon twelve o'clock in the day

no one no person

noose a loop made in a piece of rope so that when the rope is pulled the loop gets smaller

normal usual or ordinary

north the direction to your left when you face east

northern from the north or in the north

nose the part of the face that is used for breathing and smelling

nostril one of the two holes at the end of the nose for taking in air

notch a mark like a V, cut into something

note 1 a short letter
2 one sound in music

nothing not anything

notice 1 to see something and think about it
2 something fixed to a wall or a piece of board, for you to read

nought the sign for nothing, 0

noun any word that tells you what someone or something is called. *Air*, *Ann*, *speed*, *England*, and *chair* are all nouns.

nourish to feed someone well

novelty something new or unusual

now at this time

nowhere not anywhere

nozzle the part at the end of a piece of pipe where a spray of liquid or powder comes out

nude without any clothes

nudge to push someone with your elbow to make him notice something

nugget a lump of gold

nuisance someone or something that causes trouble

numb not able to feel anything

number the word or sign that tells you how many. 1, two, and 3 are numbers.

numerous many

nun one of a group of women who live together and obey rules because of the religion they believe in

nurse 1 someone whose job is to look after people who are ill or hurt
2 to hold carefully in the arms

nursery a place where very young children go to play and be looked after

nut 1 a kind of fruit that you chew after you have taken off its hard shell
2 a short piece of metal that is screwed on to the end of a bolt to make it firmer

nutmeg a hard seed that is made into a powder and used in cooking to give food a better flavour

nylon a very strong thin material for making clothes and other things

Oo

oak a large tree with seeds called acorns

oar a long pole with a flat part at one end, used for rowing a boat

oasis a place with water and trees in a desert

oath a serious promise made to God

oats a plant grown by farmers. Its seed is used for feeding animals and for making food such as porridge.

obedient willing to do what you are told to do

obey to do what you are told to do

object¹ (*say* ob-ject) anything that can be seen or touched

object² (*say* ob-ject) to say that you do not like or agree with something

oblige 1 to help and please someone
2 *to be obliged to do something*
to have to do something

oblong the shape of a door or this page (see the list of shapes on page 248)

observe 1 to watch carefully **2** to say something that you have noticed

obstacle something that is in the way

obstinate not willing to change your ideas even though they might be wrong

obstruct to be in the way so that something cannot get past

obtain to get

obvious very easy to see or understand

occasion the time when something happens
*a special **occasion***

occasionally sometimes

occupation any job or hobby

occupy 1 to live in something

2 to keep someone busy and interested

occur 1 to happen
2 to come into your mind
*An idea **occurred** to me.*

ocean a big sea

o'clock by the clock
*one **o'clock***

octopus a sea creature with eight arms

odd 1 strange
*an **odd** person*
2 not even
*Five is an **odd** number.*
3 not alike
***odd** shoes*

odour a smell

off 1 away
*They ran **off**.*
2 not on
*Turn the tap **off**.*

offend to hurt someone's feelings

offensive nasty and very annoying

*an **offensive** smell*

offer 1 to hold out something so that another person can take it if he wants it
2 to say that you are willing to do something

office a room with desks and telephones, where people work

officer someone in the army, navy, or air force, who is in charge of others

officious too ready to tell people what they ought to do

often many times

ogre a giant who eats people

oil a thick, slippery liquid. Oil is put in machines to make them work better and is burnt to make heat. Another kind of oil is used in cooking.

ointment a cream for putting on sore skin or cuts

old 1 born or made a long time ago
2 not new

old-fashioned of the kind that was usual a long time ago
***old-fashioned** clothes*

omelette eggs that are mixed together and fried

omit to leave out

once **1** one time
2 at one time

onion a round, white vegetable with a very strong flavour

only **1** no more than
only two cakes
2 one by itself
the *only* one left

onward, onwards forwards
Onward, Christian soldiers!

ooze to come slowly through a hole or small opening. Blood oozes from small cuts.

open **1** not closed
2 to make open

opening a hole or space in something

operation **1** something done by doctors to a sick person's body to make it healthy again
2 the working of a machine

opinion what you think of something

opportunity a good chance to do something

opposite **1** facing
2 something that is as different as possible from another thing. Hot is the opposite of cold.

optician someone who makes or sells spectacles

orange **1** a round, juicy fruit with thick peel and white pips
2 the colour of this fruit

orbit the path in space of something moving round the sun or a planet. The moon is in orbit round the earth.

orchard a place where a lot of fruit trees grow

orchestra a group of people who play violins and other musical instruments together

ordeal a time when you have to put up with great pain or trouble

order **1** to tell someone to do something
2 to ask for something to be brought to you
3 *in order* properly arranged

ordinary not special in any way

ore a piece of rock with metal in it

organ a large musical instrument with black and white keys like a piano, pedals, and pipes

organize **1** to get people working together to do something
2 to plan and arrange things

like parties, concerts, or holidays
*She is good at **organizing** things.*

original **1** made first, before any others
2 new and not copied from anywhere
*an **original** idea*

ornament something put in a place to make it look pretty

orphan a child whose mother and father are dead

ostrich a very large bird that cannot fly and has long legs

other not the same as this
*The **other** sweets were better.*

otherwise or else

otter a furry animal that lives near water. Otters have long tails.

otter

ought should
*I **ought** to go now.*

ounce a measure for weight

ourselves **1** we and no one else
2 *by ourselves* on our own

out **1** not in
2 not burning
*The fire has gone **out**.*

outcast someone ignored and left by his family and friends

outfit **1** clothes that are worn together
2 a set of things needed for doing something

outing a day or afternoon out somewhere
*an **outing** to the zoo*

outlaw someone long ago who had to hide, because, as a punishment, he was not protected by the law and anyone could kill him. Robin Hood was a famous outlaw.

outline a line round the edge of something, that shows its shape

outside **1** not inside
2 the surface or edges of something

outstanding unusually good
outstanding work

oval the shape of an egg (see the list of shapes on page 248)

oven the space inside a stove, where food can be baked or roasted

over **1** above or covering
2 finished
Playtime is **over**.
3 left
Is there any food **over**?
4 more than
There were **over** *40,000 at the match.*

overall something worn over other clothes to keep them clean

overboard over the side of a boat into the water
Man **overboard**!

overflow to come over the sides of a container, because there is too much in it

overhead **1** above the head
overhead wires
2 in the sky above
a plane flying **overhead**

overtake to catch up and pass someone

overturn to push or knock something over

owe to have to pay money to someone

owl a bird with large eyes that hunts smaller animals at night

own **1** to have something that belongs to you
2 *to own up* to say that you were the one who did something
3 *my own* mine and no one else's
4 *on my own* by myself

ox a large animal kept for its meat or for pulling carts
two **oxen**

oxygen the gas in the air that everyone needs to breathe in order to stay alive

oyster a sea creature that lives inside a pair of shells

Pp

pace **1** one step
2 how quickly something happens or moves

pack **1** to put things into a box, bag, or suitcase in order to move them or store them
2 a group of dogs or other animals
3 a group of Brownies or Cubs
4 a set of cards used in games

package a parcel

packet a small parcel

pad **1** sheets of writing paper joined together along one edge so that you can tear a sheet off when you need it
2 soft material folded up into a kind of cushion to protect something
3 to walk softly

paddle **1** to walk about in shallow water
I like **paddling**.
2 a thin piece of wood with a flat part at the end, used to make a canoe move

padlock a lock joined to something by a metal loop

padlock

page **1** one side of a piece of paper that is part of a book
2 a little boy who walks behind the bride at a wedding

pageant (*say* paj-ent) a kind of play done outside about something that happened long ago. A pageant has many people in it wearing different costumes.

paid see **pay**

pail a bucket

pain the feeling you have when part of your body is damaged or sick

paint **1** a coloured liquid put on the surface of something to colour it
2 to use paint to colour something

painting a picture that has been painted

pair two people, animals, or things that belong together

palace a very large house where a king, or queen, or-

140

some other very important person lives

pale **1** almost white
*a **pale** face*
2 light
*a **pale** blue sky*

palette a piece of board on which an artist mixes his colours while he is painting

paling a wooden fence

palm **1** the inside of the hand between the fingers and wrist **2** a tropical tree with large leaves and no branches

pamper to treat a person or animal too well

pancake flour, milk, and egg mixed together and fried

panda an animal found in China. Giant pandas look like large black and white bears.

pane a piece of glass in a window

panel a long, flat piece of wood or metal that is part of a door, wall, or piece of furniture

panic sudden fear that cannot be controlled

pansy a small plant with a brightly coloured flower

pant to take the short, quick breaths you take after running a lot

panther an Indian leopard

pantomime a kind of play, usually done at Christmas. It tells a fairy story and has singers and comedians in it.

pantry a small room where food is kept

pants a piece of underwear for the lower part of the body

paper **1** wet rags, straw, or tiny pieces of wood pressed and dried into very thin sheets. Paper is used for making books and wrapping up things.
2 a newspaper

parable a story in order to teach people something

parachute a large piece of cloth that opens up like an umbrella when a cord is pulled. It is tied to someone's back so that he can jump out of an aeroplane and float safely down to the ground.

parade people marching along, while other people watch them

paraffin a liquid made from oil, that is burnt to make heat

parallel lines straight lines that are always the same distance from each other

paralysed not able to move or feel anything

parcel something wrapped up ready to be carried or posted

pardon to forgive

parent 1 a person who has a child
2 an animal that has young ones

park 1 a large garden where anyone can walk or play
2 to leave a car somewhere for a time until it is needed again

parliament the group of people that makes the laws of a country

parrot a brightly coloured bird that can learn to repeat things that are said to it

parsley a green plant used in

cooking to give a stronger flavour to food

parsnip a pale yellow vegetable with a sweet taste

part anything that belongs to something bigger

particle a very tiny piece *particles* of dust

particular only this one and no other
This *particular* one is my favourite.

partner one of a pair of people who dance together or play on the same side in a game

party a group of people enjoying themselves together *a Christmas party*

pass 1 to go by
2 to give someone something he wants, but cannot reach himself *Please pass the salt.*
3 to be successful in a test *She's passed her driving test.*

passage 1 a way through
2 a corridor

passenger anyone travelling in a bus, train, ship, or aeroplane, except the driver and crew

passport special papers

printed by the government that a person has to have with him in order to go to another country

past **1** the time that has gone **2** up to and further than something
*Go **past** the school.*

paste a wet mixture used for sticking paper to things

pastime something you do or play in your free time

pastry a mixture of flour, fat, and water rolled flat and baked

pasture land covered in grass that cattle, sheep, or horses can eat

patch **1** a small piece of material put over something to mend it or protect it **2** a small piece of ground

path a very narrow way that you can go along to get somewhere

patience the ability to be patient

patient **1** someone who is ill and being looked after by a doctor **2** able to bear pain or trouble **3** able to wait for a long time without getting angry

patrol a group of soldiers or policemen who move around a place to guard it

patter to make the light, tapping sound rain makes against the window

pattern **1** a set of lines and shapes drawn on something to make it look pretty **2** anything that people copy in order to make something
*a dress **pattern***

pause to stop for a very short time

pavement the part at each side of a street for people to walk along safely

pavilion the building where people playing games such as cricket can leave their things or wait for their turn

paw an animal's foot

pay to give money in return for something
*I **paid** for the sweets last time.*

pea a tiny, round, green vegetable that grows inside a pod

peace **1** a time free from war **2** a time of quiet and rest

peaceful quiet

peach a round, soft, juicy fruit with a large stone and

a thin, yellow skin
peaches and cream

peacock a large bird with very long, brightly coloured tail feathers that it can spread out like a fan

peak **1** the top of a mountain **2** the part of a cap that sticks out in front

peal to make a loud, ringing sound

peanut a tiny, round nut that grows in a pod in the ground

pear a juicy fruit that is narrow where the stalk is

pearl a small, shiny, white ball found inside the shells of some oysters. Pearls are used for making valuable jewellery.

peat soil that can be dug up in solid pieces and burnt instead of coal

pebble a small, round stone

peck to use the beak to pick up food or push at something

peculiar strange
a *peculiar* taste

pedal a part that is pressed with the foot to make something work. A bicycle has two pedals.

pedestrian someone who is walking

peel the skin on some fruit and vegetables

peep to look quickly or secretly

peer to get very close to something to look at it

pelican a bird with a very large beak that lives on water or near to it

pellet a tiny ball of wet paper, metal, food, or medicine

pelt 1 an animal's hair and skin
2 to throw a lot of things at someone

penalty a kind of punishment

pence more than one **penny**

pencil a thin wooden stick with another coloured stick inside it, used for writing and drawing

pendant something hung round the neck on a long chain or string

pendulum a rod with a weight hanging from its end so that it swings backwards and forwards. Some clocks are worked by pendulums.

penetrate to make or find a way through something

penguin a sea bird that cannot fly and uses its short, stiff wings for swimming

penknife a small knife that folds up so that you can carry it with you safely

penny a coin
100 **pence** = £1
*She counted out six **pennies**.*

people men, women, and children

pepper a powder used to give food a stronger flavour. It can make you sneeze.

peppermint a sweet with a strong mint flavour

perch 1 anything that a bird rests on when it is not flying
2 to sit on the edge of something, like a bird on a branch

percussion instrument any musical instrument that is banged, hit, or shaken. Drums, cymbals, and tambourines are percussion instruments.

perfect so good that it cannot be made any better

perform to do something in front of an audience

performance something done in front of an audience

perfume a liquid with a very sweet smell

perhaps possibly
Perhaps it will rain tomorrow.

peril danger

perimeter the distance round the edge of something (see page 249)

period any length of time

perish　**1** to die
2 to become dry and wrinkled and no longer any use. Rubber perishes.

permanent able to last for a very long time without changing

permission words that say something is allowed

permit to allow

persist to carry on doing something no matter what happens

person a man, woman, or child

persuade to get someone to agree to something

pest any person or animal that causes a lot of trouble

pester to keep worrying someone by asking questions

petal one of the separate, coloured parts of a flower. Daisies have a lot of white petals.

petrol a liquid made from oil. Petrol is put in the engines of things such as cars and aeroplanes to make them go.

petticoat a piece of clothing worn underneath dresses and skirts

pew one of the long wooden seats in a church

phone short for **telephone**

photo, photograph a picture taken with a camera and printed on paper

phrase a group of words, such as
a coat of many colours

physical having to do with the body
physical education

piano a large musical instrument with white and black keys that are pressed with the fingers

pick　**1** to choose
2 to take something up from where it is
Pick up that sweet paper.
3 to take flowers or fruit from plants and trees
4 a pickaxe

pickaxe a heavy tool with a

long handle, for breaking up very hard ground

pickles vegetables stored in vinegar

picnic a meal eaten in the open air away from home

picture a painting, drawing, or photograph

pie meat or fruit covered with pastry and baked

piece a part of something

pier something long that is built out into the sea for people to walk on. Some piers have shops on them and places where people can enjoy themselves.

pierce to make a hole through something

pigeon a bird that can be taught to fly home from far away

pile a number of things put on top of one another

pilgrim someone who makes a journey to a holy place

pill a small, round piece of medicine

pillar a wooden or stone post that helps to hold up a building

pillion the seat on a motorbike behind the rider's seat

pillow the cushion that you rest your head on in bed

pilot 1 someone who steers an aeroplane
2 someone who steers a ship in narrow, difficult places

pimple a small, round swelling on the skin

pinafore an apron

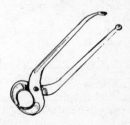

pincers a tool for holding something tightly

pinch to squeeze skin between the thumb and finger in order to hurt someone

147

pine 1 to get ill because you miss someone very much **2** a tree with cones for its seeds and clusters of leaves that look like green needles

pineapple a large fruit that grows in hot countries. It has stiff, pointed leaves and a thick skin covered in lumps.

pint a measure for liquid

pioneer 1 one of the first people to go and live in a new country **2** someone who is the first to do something

pipe 1 a tube for taking gas or water somewhere **2** a tube with a small bowl at one end, used for smoking tobacco

pirate someone on a ship, who attacks and robs other ships

pistol a small gun

pitch 1 ground marked out for cricket, football, or another game **2** a black, sticky liquid made from tar **3** to put up a tent **4** to throw

pitchfork a tool like a very large fork, for lifting hay

pity the feeling you have when you are sorry that someone is in pain or trouble

pivot a point that things swing from, spin round, or balance on. Wheels and see-saws have pivots.

pixie, pixy a kind of fairy

placard a notice

place any space where something belongs

plague a dangerous illness that spreads very quickly

plaice a sea fish that can be eaten

plain 1 not decorated **2** not pretty **3** easy to understand **4** a large area of flat ground

plait (*say* plat) **1** to twist together pieces of wool, cord, thread, straw, or hair by crossing them over and under each other **2** a long piece of plaited hair

plan 1 to decide what is going to be done **2** a map of a building or town

plane 1 short for **aeroplane 2** a tool for making wood smooth **3** a tall tree with large leaves

planet any of the worlds in

space that move round the sun. The earth is a planet. (See page 252)

plank a long, flat piece of wood

plant anything that grows out of the ground. Trees, bushes, and flowers are all plants.

plaster 1 a sticky strip of special material for covering cuts
2 a soft mixture that goes hard when it dries. Plaster is used in building, mending broken bones, and making models.

plastic something light and strong that is made in factories and used for making all kinds of things *plastic* bowls, *plastic* bags

plasticine something soft and coloured that you can make into different shapes with your hands

plate a flat dish for eating from

platform 1 a small stage
2 the place in a station where people wait beside the railway lines for a train

play 1 to be in a game
2 to make music with a musical instrument

3 a story that is acted

playground a place out of doors where children can play

playing-card one of a set of cards used in some games

playtime the time at school when children can go out to play

plead to beg for something that you want very much

pleasant pleasing
a *pleasant* holiday

please 1 to make someone happy
2 the polite word you use when you are asking for something
Please may I have another cake?

pleasure the feeling people have when they are pleased

pleat 1 a flat fold made in the material of a dress, skirt, or kilt
2 *pleated* with pleats

plenty 1 a lot of something
2 more than enough

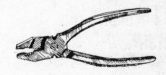

pliers a tool for holding

something tightly or for bending or breaking wire

plimsoll a light, canvas shoe with a rubber sole

plod to walk slowly and heavily

plot **1** to plan secretly
2 a small piece of ground

plough (*rhymes with* cow) a machine used on farms for digging and turning over the soil

pluck **1** to pull a feather, flower, or fruit from the place where it is growing
2 to pull at something and let it go quickly. People play guitars by plucking the strings.

plucky brave

plug **1** a part joined to a lamp or machine by wire. It fits into a place in a wall where

electricity can come into it
2 a round piece of rubber or metal that fits into a hole. It stops water running out of a bath or sink.

plum a juicy fruit with a stone in it

plumber (*say* plummer) someone who puts in and mends taps and water pipes

plume a large feather

plump fat

plunder to rob a person or place of many things by force

plunge **1** to jump suddenly into water
2 to put something suddenly into water

plural any word when it is written differently to show that it means more than one. *Cakes, children, ladies, mice,* and *monkeys* are all plurals.

plus add. Three plus three is six, $3 + 3 = 6$.

plywood a kind of wood made from thin sheets of wood glued together

pneumonia (*say* new-monia) a serious illness that makes it painful to breathe

poach **1** to cook an egg in

boiling water or steam without its shell
2 to hunt animals that are on someone else's land

pocket a part like a small bag, sewn into some clothes

pod a long seed case that grows on some plants. Peas grow inside pods.

poem a piece of writing with a special rhythm. Poems are usually written out in short lines.

poet someone who writes poetry

poetry poems

point **1** the sharp end of things such as pins and pencils
2 a mark scored in a game
3 to show where something is by holding out your finger towards it
4 to aim a weapon

pointed with a point at the end

poison any liquid, powder, or plant that will kill or harm you if you swallow it

poisonous likely to harm you because it contains poison
poisonous berries

poke to push hard with the end of your finger or a stick

poker a metal rod for poking a fire

polar bear a very large, white bear that lives in the Arctic

pole **1** a long, round stick of wood or metal
2 either of the two ends of a magnet
3 *North pole* the place that is the furthest north in the world
4 *South pole* the place that is the furthest south in the world

police the people whose job is to catch criminals and make sure that the law is kept. There are thousands of **policemen** and **policewomen** in Britain.

polish to rub the surface of something to make it shine

polite having good manners
a *polite* boy

pollen the yellow powder inside a flower. Pollen helps to make seeds.

poncho

poncho a piece of cloth with a hole in the middle for the head, worn over clothes

pond a very small lake

ponder to think about something carefully

pony a small horse

poodle a kind of dog with curly hair often cut very short on some parts of its body

pool a small area of water

poor **1** having very little money
a **poor** family
2 bad
poor work, **poor** crops

poplar a tall, straight tree

poppy a bright red flower often found growing near corn

popular liked by a lot of people

population the number of people who live in a place

porch a small place with a roof, in front of the door of a building

pork meat from a pig

porpoise a sea animal like a small whale

porpoise

porridge a hot food made from oats boiled in water and eaten at breakfast

port a large place where ships can stay safely in the water when they are not at sea

portable able to be carried about
a **portable** television

porter someone whose job is to carry other people's luggage at places like hotels and railway stations

portion the part or amount given to you

portrait a picture of a person

posh very smart

position **1** the place where something is or should be
2 how the body and its parts are arranged
a sitting **position**

positive completely sure

possess to own

possible able to happen or to be done

post **1** an upright pole fixed in the ground
2 to send a letter, parcel, or card

postcard a piece of card that you can write a message on and post

poster a large notice for everyone to read

postman someone who collects and delivers letters and parcels

post office a place that sells stamps and deals with letters and parcels

postpone to put off until later

potato a vegetable dug out of the ground
baked **potatoes**

potion a drink with medicine or poison in it

pottery cups, plates, and other things made out of baked clay

pouch **1** a small bag
2 a kind of pocket that some animals have in their skin. Hamsters have pouches inside their cheeks.

pouffe (rhymes with roof)
a low seat that is like a large, firm cushion

poultry birds kept for their meat and eggs

pounce to attack something by jumping on it suddenly

pound **1** a measure for weight
2 a measure for money, also written £
£1 = 100 pence
3 to beat very hard with the fists
4 to crush something by hitting it very hard

pour **1** to hold a container so that liquid runs out of it quickly
2 **to pour with rain** to rain hard

pout to stick out your lips when you are not pleased

powder anything that is very dry and made up of many separate tiny bits, like flour or dust

power **1** the ability to do something
2 strength

powerful very strong or important

practical **1** able to do useful things
2 likely to be useful

*a **practical** idea*

practice something you keep doing in order to get better at it
*piano **practice***

practise to do something over and over again in order to get better at doing it

prairie a very large area of flat ground covered in grass, in North America

praise to say that someone or something is very good

pram a kind of cot on wheels for a baby

prance to jump about in a very lively way
*a **prancing** horse*

pray to talk to God

prayer talking to God

preach to speak to other people just as a priest does in church

precious very valuable
*a **precious** jewel*

precipice a very steep part of a mountain or rock

prefer to like one person or thing more than another person or thing

pregnant expecting a baby

prehistoric belonging to a

time very long ago
prehistoric animals

preparations things that are done to get ready for something

prepare to get something ready

present[1] (*say* prez-ent)
1 something given to someone
2 the time now
*Our teacher is away at **present**.*
3 here
*All **present** and correct, sir!*

present[2] (*say* pri-zent)
to give someone a prize or gift in front of other people

presently soon

preserve **1** to keep safe
2 to do things to food so that it will not go bad

president someone chosen to rule a country that does not have a king or queen

press **1** to push hard on something
2 to make something flat or smooth by pushing hard on it

pressure **1** pressing on something
2 how much one thing is pressing on another

pretend to make it seem that

something not true is true
*He **pretended** he was ill.*

pretty pleasant to look at
*a **pretty** girl, a **pretty** dress*

prevent to stop something from happening

previous coming before this one
*the **previous** week*

prey 1 any animal hunted and eaten by another animal
2 a bird of prey a bird that hunts and eats other animals

price the amount of money you have to pay for something

priceless very valuable

prick to make a tiny hole in something

prickle a sharp part like a thorn

pride the feeling people have when they are proud

priest 1 someone who serves God by being in charge of a church
2 a man who leads people in their religion

primary school the school you go to when you are about five years old

Prime Minister the most important person in the government

primrose a small, pale yellow flower that comes out early in the spring

prince the son of a king or queen

princess 1 the daughter of a king or queen
2 the wife of a prince

principal most important or chief

principle an important rule

print 1 to write with letters that are not joined together
2 to use a machine that presses words and pictures on to paper. Books, newspapers, and magazines are printed.

prison a place where criminals are kept as a punishment

prisoner 1 someone who has been captured
2 someone in prison

private 1 not open to everyone
*a **private** road*
2 not known by other people
*a **private** thought*

prize something that is won

probable likely to be true or to happen

problem something that is difficult to understand or to answer

proceed to go on

procession a group of people moving along in a long line

prod to push something with the end of a finger or stick

produce **1** to make
2 to bring something out so that it can be seen

producer the person in charge of the acting of a play

profit the extra money got by selling something for more than it cost to buy or make

programme **1** a talk, play, or show on the radio or television
2 a list for people in an audience telling them about what they will see or hear

progress **1** moving forward
2 getting better

prohibit to say that people must not do something

project **1** finding out as much as you can about something interesting and writing about it
a **project** on flight
2 a plan

promenade a kind of road by the sea where people can walk

promise to say that you will certainly do or not do something
He's always **promising** us things.

prompt done straight away

prong one of the thin, pointed parts on the end of a fork

pronounce to say a sound or word in a certain way

proof something that shows that an idea is true

prop **1** a long piece of wood or metal put underneath something to support it
2 to support one thing by leaning it against another thing
The ladder was **propped** up against the wall.

propel to drive forward

propeller a set of blades that

spin round. Propellers are fixed to aeroplanes, helicopters, and ships to make them move.

proper correct
*in the **proper** place*

property things that belong to someone

prophet someone who tells people what is going to happen

prosecute to make someone go to court so that he can be punished if he has done wrong
*Trespassers will be **prosecuted**.*

prosper to become successful or rich

protect to keep safe from danger

protection something that protects

protest to say or show that you think what someone else is saying or doing is wrong

proud 1 full of the idea that you are better or more important than you really are 2 very pleased because you or someone belonging to you has done well
*He is **proud** of his sister.*

prove to show that an idea is true

proverb something often said in order to help people, such as 'A stitch in time saves nine.'

provide to give something that is needed

prowl to move about like an animal looking for something to kill and eat

prune 1 a dried plum 2 to cut parts off a tree or bush

pry to try to find out about something that has nothing to do with you

psalm (*say* sarm) one of the hymns in the Bible

public 1 all the people 2 open to everyone

pudding something sweet made to be eaten after the main part of a meal
*Christmas **pudding***

puddle a small pool of dirty water

puff 1 a small amount of breath, wind, or smoke 2 to blow out puffs of smoke or air 3 **puffed** out of breath

puffin a sea bird with a large

157

orange and blue beak

pull to get hold of something and make it come towards you

pulley a wheel with rope round it, used for lifting heavy things

pullover a jersey

pulp anything that has been made soft and wet
fruit **pulp**, *paper* **pulp**

pulpit the high wooden desk in a church, where the priest stands to talk to the people

pulse the throbbing that can be felt at the wrist as the blood is pumped around inside the body

pump **1** a machine that pushes liquid or air through pipes
2 to push air or liquid into something
Pump *up that flat tyre.*

pumpkin

pumpkin a very large, round fruit with a hard yellow skin

punch **1** to hit with the fist
2 a tool for making holes in paper or leather

punctual exactly on time

punctuation marks such as commas and full stops put into a piece of writing to make it easier to read

puncture a hole in a tyre

punish to make someone who has done wrong suffer, so that he will not want to do wrong again

punishment something done to punish someone

pupil **1** someone who has a teacher
2 the black spot at the centre of the eye

puppet **1** a kind of doll whose head and limbs can be moved by strings and rods
2 a kind of doll with a body like a glove, so that you can move its head and arms with your fingers

puppy a very young dog

purchase to buy

pure with nothing else mixed with it

pure *water*

purpose what someone means to do

purr to make the sound a cat makes when it is very pleased

purse a small bag for holding money

pursue to run after someone and try to catch him

push to use your hands to move something away from you

put to move something into a place
*I **put** everything away yesterday.*

putty something soft and sticky that sets hard, used for fixing glass into windows

puzzle 1 a game or question that is difficult to work out and makes you think a lot
2 to make someone think very hard to find the answer
*a **puzzling** question*

pyjamas trousers and a jacket worn in bed

pylon a metal tower that holds up high electric cables

pyramid 1 a large, stone building made by the ancient Egyptians to hold the body of

pylon

a dead king or queen. Pyramids have sloping sides that meet in a point at the top.
2 the shape of a pyramid (see the list of shapes on page 249)

python a very large snake

Qq

quack to make the sound a duck makes

quail 1 a wild bird that can be eaten
2 to look frightened

quaint unusual but pleasant
*a **quaint** cottage*

quake to shake because you are very frightened

quality how good or bad something is

quantity an amount

quarrel to speak angrily to someone or fight with him, because he does not agree with you

quarry 1 a place where people cut stone out of the ground so that it can be used for building
2 an animal that is being hunted

quarter one of the four equal parts something can be divided into. It can also be written as $\frac{1}{4}$.

quay (*say* key)
a place where ships can be loaded and unloaded

queen 1 a woman who has been crowned as ruler of a country
2 a king's wife

queer very strange
a **queer** feeling

quench 1 to put an end to someone's thirst
The tea **quenched** her thirst.
2 to use water to put out a fire

query (*say* queery)
a question that you ask about something, because you think it might be wrong

quest a long search

question something that you ask when you want to find out or get something

queue (*say* cue)
a line of people waiting for something

quick 1 done in less time than usual
a **quick** snack
2 fast
Be **quick**!

quiet 1 without any noise
2 not loud
a **quiet** voice

quill 1 a big feather from a bird's wing or tail
2 a pen made from a feather

quilt a bed cover like a large, flat cushion. It has lines of stitching across it to keep the filling in place.

quite 1 completely
I'm **quite** sure.
2 **quite big** big, but not enormous

quiver 1 to shake because you are very cold or frightened
2 a bag for carrying arrows

quiver

quiz a kind of game in which people try to answer a lot of questions in order to show how much they know
two **quizzes**

Rr

rabbit a furry animal with long ears. Rabbits live in holes they have dug in the ground.

race a competition to find the fastest

rack a set of bars made into a shelf or something else that people can put things on
a luggage **rack**

racket **1** a kind of bat with a wooden or metal frame and string stretched across it in a criss-cross pattern
a tennis **racket**
2 a lot of loud noise

radiant **1** bright
radiant sunshine
2 looking very happy
a **radiant** *smile*

radiate to give out heat or light

radiator **1** a metal container or a set of pipes that gives out heat in a room
2 the part inside a car for keeping the engine cool

radio a machine that changes programmes and messages sent through the air into sound so that people can listen to them

radish a small, hard, round, red vegetable, eaten raw in salads

radius the distance from the centre of a circle to the edge
two **radii** (see page 248)

raffia a kind of soft straw made from the leaves of palm trees and used for weaving mats and bags

raffle a kind of sale held to get money for something. People buy tickets with numbers on them and certain numbers win prizes.

raft something flat made of

pieces of wood joined together and used instead of a boat

rafter one of the long, sloping pieces of wood that hold up a roof

rage great anger

raid a sudden attack on a place

rail **1** a bar or rod
2 a long metal bar that is part of a railway line

railings a fence made of metal bars

railway the set of metal bars that trains travel on

rain drops of water that fall from the sky

rainbow the curved band of different colours seen in the sky when the sun shines through the rain

raincoat a coat made of waterproof material for keeping you dry when it rains

raise **1** to lift up or make something higher
2 to gather together the money or people needed for something

raisin a dried grape used in cooking

rake a tool used in the garden. It has a long handle and a row of short spikes.

rally a large number of people who have come together for a big meeting

ram **1** a male sheep
2 to push one thing very hard into another thing

ramble a long walk in the country

ran see **run**

ranch a large American farm with a lot of cattle or horses

random *at random* without any plan or aim

rang see **ring**

rank **1** a title or job that shows how important someone is. The rank of general is higher than the rank of captain.
2 a row of people

ransack to search everywhere for something and leave things looking very untidy

ransom money paid so that a prisoner can be set free

rap to knock quickly and loudly

rapid very quick

rare not often found. Pandas are rare animals.

rascal **1** a naughty child
2 someone who is not honest

rash **1** done in a rush without any thought about what might happen
a **rash** action
2 red spots or patches that suddenly come on the skin
a measles **rash**

raspberry a soft, sweet, red berry

rate how quickly something happens or is done

rather **1** fairly
It's **rather** cold.
2 more willingly

I'd **rather** have a cake.

rattle **1** to make quick, hard noises by shaking something
2 a baby's toy that rattles

rave to talk in a very excited or enthusiastic way

raven a large, black bird

ravenous very hungry

ravine (say rav-<u>een</u>) a very deep, narrow space between mountains

raw not cooked

ray a thin line of light
the sun's **rays**

razor a very thin, sharp blade. Men shave their faces with razors.

reach **1** to stretch out the hand in order to touch something
He **reached** for a cake.
2 to arrive at a place

read¹ (*say* reed)
to be able to say and understand words that are written down
*Can you **read** this?*
*I've **read** this before.*

read² (*say* red)
see **read¹**

ready 1 able and willing to do something at once
*Are you **ready** yet?*
2 fit to be used at once
*Everything is **ready**.*

real not a copy
*a **real** diamond*

realize to come to understand something clearly

really truly
*Is it **really** snowing?*

realm (*rhymes with* helm)
the land a king or queen rules

reap to cut down and gather in the corn when it is ready

rear 1 the back part of something
2 to look after children or young animals until they are big
3 to stand on the back legs and lift the front legs into the air, like a dog begging

reason anything that explains why something has happened

reasonable 1 fair
*a **reasonable** price*
2 sensible

rebel¹ (*say* ri-<u>bell</u>)
to decide not to obey the people in charge
*The soldiers **rebelled**.*

rebel² (*say* <u>reb</u>-el)
someone who rebels

recall to remember

receive to get something that has been given or sent to you

recent made or done a short time ago

recipe (*say* resip-ee)
instructions that tell you how to cook something

recite to say a poem or something else that you have learnt by heart

reckless likely to do silly or dangerous things. Reckless people do things without thinking or caring about what might happen.

reckon 1 to count or add up
2 to think something and feel sure it is right

recognize to know who someone is because you have seen him before

record 1 a flat, round piece

of black plastic that makes music or other sounds while it is turning round on a record-player
2 the best that has been done so far in a sport or hobby
*He broke the world **record** in that race.*
3 facts that are written down and kept

recorder a wooden musical instrument shaped like a tube, that you blow

record-player a machine that makes sounds come out of records

recover **1** to get better after being ill
2 to get something back that you have lost

recreation hobbies or games people like playing in their spare time

rectangle the shape of a postcard (see the list of shapes on page 248)

reduce to make smaller or less

reed a plant with a strong stem that grows near water

reef a line of rocks just below or just above the surface of the sea

reek to have a strong smell that is not pleasant

reel **1** a round piece of wood or metal that cotton, string, or film is wound round
2 a Scottish dance
3 to lose your balance because you feel dizzy

refer **1** to say a little about something while talking about other things
*She **referred** to the match in assembly.*
2 to look in a book for information

referee someone who makes sure that the players in a game keep to the rules

reference book a book that gives you information. Dictionaries are reference books.

reflect **1** to send back light from a shiny surface. Water often reflects the light of the sun.
2 to show a picture of something, as a mirror does

reflection a picture seen in a mirror or water

refresh to make a tired person feel fresh and strong again
*a **refreshing** drink*

refreshments drinks and snacks

refrigerator a kind of metal cupboard that keeps food and drink cold and fresh

refuse[1] (*say* ri-<u>fuse</u>)
1 to say you will not do something you have been asked to do
2 to say you do not want what someone is offering you

refuse[2] (*say* <u>ref</u>-yooss) rubbish

regard **1** to look at
2 to think of someone or something in a certain way

regiment a large, organized group of soldiers

region a part of a country or the world

register an important book with a list of names and addresses in it
*a school **register***

regret the feeling you have when you are sorry about something

regular **1** usual
2 always happening at certain times
***regular** meals*

rehearsal a practice for a concert or play

rehearse to practise something before it is done in front of an audience

reign **1** to be king or queen
2 the time when someone is king or queen

reindeer a kind of deer that lives in very cold countries

reins the two long straps used for guiding a horse

rejoice to be very happy about something

relation a relative

relative someone in the same family as you

relax to rest the body by letting it become less stiff

relay race a race between teams in which each person does part of the distance

release to set someone free

relent to be less angry than you were going to be

reliable able to be trusted
*a **reliable** person*

relic something very old that was left by people who lived long ago

relief the feeling you have when you are no longer in trouble, pain, or danger

relieved happy because you

are no longer in trouble, pain, or danger

religion what people believe about God and the way they worship

reluctant not willing to do something

rely to trust someone or something to help you
*The blind man **relied** on his dog.*

remain **1** to stay
2 to be left behind

remainder what is left over

remark to say something that you have thought or noticed

remarkable so unusual that you remember it
*a **remarkable** story*

remedy something that cures an illness

remember to be able to bring something into your mind when you want to

remind to make or help someone remember something

remote far away

removal van a van for moving the things inside a house to a different house

remove to take something away

rent an amount of money paid every week or month for the use of something that belongs to another person

repair to mend

repeat to say or do the same thing again

repent to be very sorry about something you have said or done

replace **1** to put something back
2 to take the place of another person or thing

reply to answer

report to tell or write news

represent **1** to speak or do things in place of another person or a group of people
2 to be a picture or model of something

reproach to tell someone how sad or angry you are that he has done wrong

reptile an animal with cold blood that creeps or crawls. Snakes, crocodiles, and tortoises are all reptiles

reputation the things everyone says or thinks about a person

request to ask politely for something

require to need

rescue to save from danger

resemble to look or sound like another person or thing

reserve **1** to keep for later **2** someone ready to take part in a game if a member of the team cannot play

reservoir a place where a very large amount of water is stored

resist to fight against something and not give way

resolve to decide

respect the feeling you have for someone you like and admire

responsible in charge and likely to take the blame if anything goes wrong

rest **1** to lie down, lean against something, or sit without doing anything **2** the part that is left **3** the other people or things *You stay, but the **rest** can go.*

restaurant a place where you can buy a meal and eat it

restore **1** to put something back **2** to make something as good as it was before

result **1** anything that happens because of other things that have happened **2** the score or marks at the end of a game, competition, or test

retire to stop working because you are too old or ill *My grandmother is **retiring** soon.*

retreat to go back because it is too dangerous to carry on

return **1** to come back to a place **2** to give something back

reveal to let something be seen or known

revenge a wish to hurt someone because he has hurt you or one of your friends

reverse **1** the opposite side or way **2** to go backwards in a car

revolt **1** to say that you will not obey the people in charge **2** *revolting* so nasty that you feel sick

revolution a great struggle to get rid of the government by force and put a new kind of government in its place

revolver a small gun that can be fired several times without having to be loaded again

reward a present given to someone because of something he has done

rhinoceros a very large, heavy animal found in Africa and Asia. Rhinoceroses have horns on their noses.

rhubarb a plant with pink stalks that are cooked and eaten with sugar

rhyme (*say* rime)
A word that has the same sound at the end as another word. *Bat* and *mat* are rhymes and so are *batter* and *matter*.

rhythm (*say* ri-them)
the pattern made in music or poetry by the strong and weak sounds

rib one of the curved bones above the waist

ribbon a strip of nylon, silk, or some other material

rice shiny white seeds that are cooked in liquid
rice pudding

rich having a lot of money
a *rich* miser

rick a neat pile of straw or hay

ridden see **ride**

riddle a question or puzzle that is a joke, such as
Why do Swiss cows have bells?
Because their horns don't work.

ride **1** to sit on a horse or bicycle and control it as it moves along
Have you ridden before?
I rode her pony yesterday.
Do you like riding?
2 to travel in a car, bus, or train

ridge a long, narrow part higher than the rest, like the line along the top of a roof

ridiculous so silly that people might laugh at it
a *ridiculous* answer

rifle a long gun that is held against the shoulder when it is fired

right   **1** on the side opposite the left. Most people hold a knife in their right hand and a fork in their left hand.
2 correct
the **right** answer
3 fair
It is not **right** to cheat.
4 completely
Turn it **right** round.

right-handed using the right hand to write and do other important things, because you find it easier than using the left hand

rim the edge round the top of a round container or round the outside of a wheel

rind the skin on bacon, cheese, or fruit

ring   **1** a circle
2 a circle of thin metal worn on the finger
3 to make a bell sound
I've **rung** your bell twice.
4 to telephone
He **rang** up the police an hour ago.

ring-master the person with a top hat and a whip who is in charge of what happens in the circus ring

rink an area of ice or ground for skating on

rinse to wash something in clean water

riot a large group of people shouting and fighting

rip to tear

ripe ready to be gathered or eaten
ripe fruit

ripen   **1** to become ripe
2 to make ripe

ripple a tiny movement on the surface of water

rise   **1** to go upwards
The sun has already **risen**.
Prices are **rising**.
2 to get up
They all **rose** as she came in.

risk the chance of danger

rival someone trying to win the same prize as you are

river a large stream

road a way with a hard surface made for people, animals, and traffic to go along

roam to move around without trying to get anywhere

roar to make the loud, deep sound a lion makes

roast to cook meat or vegetables inside the oven with fat

robber someone who steals and is ready to hurt people who get in his way

robbery taking things by force from other people
*a bank **robbery***

robin a small, brown bird with a red patch on its front

robot a machine that can move and behave like a person

rock **1** something very hard and heavy that is part of the mountains, the hills, and the ground
2 a hard sweet shaped like a stick and sold at the seaside
3 to move gently backwards and forwards or from side to side

rocket **1** a firework joined to a stick. Rockets shoot high into the air when they are lit.
2 a tall, metal tube that is shot into space by hot gases rushing out of it at the bottom

rod a long, thin, round piece of wood or metal

rode see **ride**

rogue **1** a naughty child
2 someone who is not honest

roll **1** a cylinder made by rolling something up
2 a very small loaf of bread
3 to turn over and over like a ball moving along the ground

roller **1** a heavy cylinder rolled over things to make them flat or smooth
2 a small cylinder put in hair to curl it

roller-skate a set of small wheels that fit under each shoe and make you able to move quickly and smoothly over the ground

rolling-pin a wooden cylinder rolled over pastry to make it flat

rompers a piece of clothing worn by babies that covers the whole of the body

roof the part that covers the top of a building

room **1** one of the spaces with walls round it inside a building. Bathrooms, kitchens, and lounges are rooms.

2 enough space for something

roost the place where a bird rests at night

root the part of a plant that grows under the ground

rope a lot of strong threads twisted together

rose **1** a flower with a sweet smell and thorns on its stem
2 see **rise**

rosy coloured like a pink or red rose

rot to go soft or bad so that it cannot be used. Fruit and wood rot.

rotten **1** very bad
a **rotten** player
2 so soft or bad that it cannot be used
a **rotten** apple, **rotten** wood

rough **1** not smooth
rough wood
2 not gentle
a **rough** boy
3 not exact
a **rough** guess

round **1** shaped like a circle or ball
2 on all sides of something
a fence **round** the field

roundabout **1** a machine with seats that moves round and round. People can ride on roundabouts at fairs or in parks.
2 a place where roads meet and all traffic has to go round in the same direction

rounders a game played outside between two teams with a small ball and a bat like a heavy stick

rouse **1** to wake someone up
2 to make someone excited about something

route (say root)
the way you have to go to get to a place

rove to travel around from place to place

row[1] (rhymes with toe)
1 people or things in a straight line
2 to use oars to make a boat move

row[2] (rhymes with how)
1 a quarrel
2 a lot of noise

royal belonging to a king or queen
the **royal** family

rubber **1** a strong material that stretches, bends, and bounces. Rubber is used for making tyres, balls, elastic bands, and many other things.

2 a piece of rubber for rubbing out pencil marks

rubbish **1** things that are not wanted or needed
2 nonsense
*You're talking **rubbish**!*

ruby a red jewel

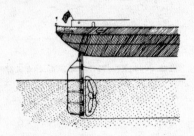

rudder a flat part fixed to the end of a ship or aeroplane and used to steer it

rude not polite

rugged (*say* rug-id) rough and full of rocks
***rugged** countryside*

ruin **1** to spoil something completely
2 a building that has fallen down

rule **1** something that everyone ought to obey
2 to be in charge of a country and the people who live there
3 to draw a straight line with a ruler

ruler **1** someone who rules a country or empire
2 a strip of wood, metal, or plastic with straight edges, used for measuring and drawing straight lines

rumble to make the deep, heavy sound thunder makes

rumour something that a lot of people are saying, although it might not be true

run to use the legs to move quickly
*He saw the bull and **ran**.*

rung **1** one of the short bars on a ladder
2 see **ring**

rush **1** to move very quickly
2 a plant with a thin stem that grows in marshes

rusk a kind of biscuit for babies to chew

rust a rough, red surface that covers iron that has got damp or wet

rustle to make the light sounds dry leaves make when they are blown by the wind

rut a groove made in the ground by wheels going over it many times

rye a plant grown by farmers. Its seed is used for feeding animals and making some kinds of bread.

Ss

sack 1 a large bag made of strong, rough material
*a **sack** of potatoes*
2 **to get the sack** to lose your job

sacred very holy

sacrifice 1 to give up something you like very much in order to help someone
2 a gift offered to God

saddle a seat put on a horse's back or on a bicycle so that you can ride it

safari a journey made by people in order to hunt or look at lions and other wild animals

safe 1 free from danger
2 a strong box where money or valuable things can be kept safe from thieves

safety a time or place free from danger
*The fireman carried her to **safety**.*

sag to go down in the middle because something heavy is pressing on it
*The chair **sagged** under his weight.*

said see **say**

sail 1 a large piece of strong cloth joined to a boat. The wind blows into the sail and makes the boat move.
2 to travel in a boat

sailor a member of a ship's crew

saint a very holy person
St Nicholas

sake **for someone's sake** to help or please someone
*Please do it **for my sake**.*

salad a mixture of vegetables eaten raw or cold

salary money paid to someone each month for the work he does

sale 1 the selling of things
2 a time when things in a shop are sold at reduced prices

salmon a large fish with pink flesh that is eaten

salt a white powder put on food to make it taste better

salute to touch your forehead with your hand, as soldiers do to show respect

same not different in any way
*My dress is the **same** as yours.*

sample a small amount that

shows what something is like
free **samples**

sand the tiny bits of rock that cover deserts and ground next to the sea

sandal a kind of light shoe with straps that go round the foot

sandwich two slices of bread and butter with a different food between them
a ham **sandwich**

sang see **sing**

sank see **sink**

sap the liquid inside a plant

sapling a young tree

sardine a small sea fish

sari a kind of long dress worn by Indian women and girls

sash a strip of material tied round the waist of a dress

sat see **sit**

satchel a bag worn over the shoulder or on the back, for carrying books to and from school

satellite something that moves in space around earth or another planet. The moon is a satellite of the earth.

satin smooth cloth that is very shiny on one side

satisfactory good enough
satisfactory *work*

satisfy to be good enough to please someone

sauce a thick liquid put on food to make it taste better

saucepan a metal pan with a handle and lid used for cooking things on top of a stove

saucer a kind of small plate for putting a cup on

sausage a skin tube stuffed with tiny pieces of meat and bread

savage wild and fierce
a **savage** *animal*

save **1** to free someone or something from danger **2** to keep something so that it can be used later
We're **saving** *silver paper for the blind.*

saw **1** a tool with a wide, thin

blade that is moved
backwards and forwards
across a piece of wood to cut
it
2 to use a saw to cut a piece
of wood
The wood was **sawn** *in two.*
I **sawed** *it in half yesterday.*
3 see **see**

sawdust a powder that
comes from wood when it is
cut with a saw

sawed, sawn see **saw**

say to use the voice to make
words
He **said** *he hadn't seen it.*

saying something wise that is
often said, such as 'A rolling
stone gathers no moss.'

scab hard, brown skin that
covers a cut or graze while it
is getting better

scabbard a cover for the
blade of a sword

scaffolding planks fixed to
poles and put round a
building so that workmen can
stand on them while they are
painting or mending it

scald to burn yourself with
very hot liquid

scales **1** a weighing
machine
a pair of **scales**
2 thin pieces of skin or bone
that cover the outside of
animals such as fish and
snakes

scalp the skin covering the top
of the head where the hair
grows

scamper to run about quickly.
Small dogs scamper.

scar the mark left on the skin
by a cut or burn after it has
healed

scarce **1** not enough of
something
Water is **scarce** *in deserts.*
2 not often seen or found

scare to frighten
Stop **scaring** *me!*

scarecrow something that
looks like a person and is put
in a field to frighten away
birds so that they will not eat
the crops

scarf a piece of material worn

round the neck or head
*two **scarves***

scarlet bright red

scatter to throw small things
so that they fall in many
different places

scene **1** the place where
something happens
*the **scene** of the crime*
2 part of a play

scenery **1** painted curtains
and screens put on a stage
to make it look like another
place
2 things such as hills, rivers,
and trees that you can see
around you when you are
out in the country

scent **1** a liquid with a sweet
smell
2 a pleasant smell
*the **scent** of roses*
3 an animal's smell
*a fox's **scent***

scholarship money given to
someone clever in order to
help him to go on studying

school the place where
children go to learn

schooner (*say* skooner)
a ship with sails and at least
two masts

science knowledge about the
world that people get by

schooner

studying things and testing
ideas about the way they
work

scientific having to do with
science
*a **scientific** experiment*

scientist someone who
studies science

scissors a tool for cutting that
has two blades joined
together
*a pair of **scissors***

scoff to make fun of
something

scold to tell someone off
angrily

scoop **1** a deep spoon for
lifting up and measuring out
potato or ice cream
2 to use a tool or your arms
or hands to gather things
together and lift them up

scooter **1** a toy with two
wheels that is ridden. You

stand on it with one foot and push the other foot against the ground to make it move.
2 a kind of motorbike with a very small engine

scorch to make something so hot that it goes brown

score **1** to get a goal or point in a game
2 the number of points or goals each side has at the end of a game
3 twenty
three **score** *years and ten*

scorn to show that you think someone or something is not worth bothering about

scout a soldier sent to spy on the enemy

Scout a boy who is a member of the Scout Association

scowl to make your face look unhappy and angry

scramble **1** to use your hands and feet to climb up or down something
2 *scrambled eggs* eggs mixed with milk and cooked in butter

scrap **1** a small piece
2 rubbish

scrape to rub with something rough or sharp

scratch **1** to damage

something by rubbing your nails or a sharp point over it
2 to rub your skin to stop it itching

scrawl to write with big, untidy letters

scream to make a loud cry that shows that you are very frightened or in pain

screech to make a loud, shrill sound that is not pleasant. Some owls screech.

screen **1** a smooth surface on which films or television programmes are shown
2 a kind of thin wall or a set of curtains on rails, that can be moved about. Screens are used for hiding things or protecting people.

screw **1** a kind of nail that is put into a hole and twisted in order to fasten things tightly together
2 to turn or twist something

screwdriver a tool for turning a screw until it fits tightly into something

scribble to write or draw quickly and untidily

scripture a sacred book such as the Bible

scroll a book written on a long sheet of paper that is rolled up

scrub to rub something very hard with a brush dipped in soap and water

sculptor an artist who makes shapes and patterns in stone, wood, clay, or metal

scurry to run with fast, little steps. Mice scurry.

scuttle **1** to move quickly like a frightened mouse **2** a kind of bucket in which coal is kept

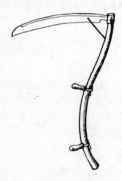

scythe (*say* sythe) a tool with a long curved blade for cutting grass

sea a very large area of salt water

sea-gull a kind of sea bird

seal **1** a furry animal that lives in the sea and on land **2** to close something by sticking two parts together a ***sealed*** envelope

seam the line where two pieces of cloth are sewn together

search to look very carefully for something

searchlight a strong light that can be pointed in any direction

seaside a place by the sea where people go to enjoy themselves

season **1** one of the four parts of the year. Spring, summer, autumn, and winter are the names of the seasons. **2** to put salt or pepper on food to make it taste better

seat a chair or stool or anything else that people sit on

seaweed a plant that grows in the sea

second **1** a very small measure for time *60* ***seconds*** *= 1 minute* **2** coming after the first ***second*** prize

secret something that must be kept hidden from other people

secretary someone whose job is to type letters, answer

179

the telephone, and arrange things in an office

section a part of something

secure safe or firm

see to use your eyes to get to know something
I **saw** an accident this morning.
Have you **seen** my cat anywhere?

seed a tiny thing put into the ground so that a plant can grow from it

seek to try to find
We **sought** for him everywhere, but could not find him.

seem to make people think something is true or likely
He **seems** brave but he isn't.

seen see **see**

see-saw a plank balanced in the middle so that someone can sit on each end and make it go up and down

seize to take hold of something suddenly

seldom not often
I **seldom** cry

select to choose

self everything in a person that makes him different from anyone else

selfish only bothered about yourself and what you want

sell to give in return for money
I **sold** my bike yesterday

semicircle half of a circle (see the list of shapes on page 248)

semolina small, hard pieces of wheat cooked with milk to make a pudding

send to make a person or thing go somewhere
She **sent** me a card last week.

senior older or more important

sensation **1** anything that you can feel happening to yourself
2 something very exciting that happens

sense **1** the power to see, hear, smell, feel, or taste
2 the ability to know what it is best to do or say

sensible wise
a **sensible** person
a **sensible** idea

sensitive easily hurt or offended
sensitive skin
a **sensitive** person

sent see **send**

sentence a group of words

that belong together. A written sentence always begins with a capital letter and ends with a question mark like this ?, an exclamation mark like this !, or a full stop like this .
*Is this a **sentence**? Yes, it is.*

sentry a soldier who is guarding a building

separate not joined to anything

sequin one of the tiny, round, shiny things sewn on clothes to decorate them

sergeant a soldier or police officer who is in charge of other soldiers or police officers

serial a story told in parts
*a television **serial***

series **1** a full set
*a **series** of stamps*
2 a number of things that are similar and come one after the other
*a television **series***

serious **1** careful and thoughtful
*a **serious** boy*
2 not silly or funny
*a **serious** talk*
3 very bad
*a **serious** accident*

serpent a large snake

servant someone whose job is to work in someone else's house

serve **1** to work for someone
2 to sell things to people in a shop
3 to give food out at a meal

serviette a square of cloth or paper for keeping you clean while you eat

session a time spent doing one thing

set **1** a group of people or things that belong together
*a **set** of drums*
2 to become solid or hard
*The jelly has **set** very quickly*
3 to put
4 **to set off** to start
*They **set off** for home.*

settee a long, comfortable seat with a back, for more than one person

settle **1** to get comfortable in a place and stay there
*We're **settling** down in our new home now.*
2 to decide

several more than a few but not a lot

severe **1** not kind or gentle
*a **severe** teacher*

181

2 very bad
*a **severe** cold*

sew (*say* so)
to use a needle and cotton to join pieces of cloth together
*He has **sewn** his badge on.*

sex one of the two groups, either male or female, that all people and animals belong to

shabby looking worn and faded
***shabby** clothes*

shack a rough hut

shade 1 a place that is darker and cooler than other places, because the light of the sun cannot get to it
2 how light or dark a colour is
3 to make part of a drawing darker than the rest

shadow the dark shape that you see on the wall or ground near something that is standing in the way of the light

shaft 1 a long, thin pole
*the **shaft** of an arrow*
2 a deep, narrow hole
*a mine **shaft***

shaggy with long, untidy hair
*a **shaggy** dog*

shake to move quickly up and down or from side to side
*I **shook** with fear, when I saw it.*
*The trees were **shaken** by the wind.*

shallow not deep
***shallow** water*

shame the feeling you have when you are upset because you have done wrong

shameful so bad that it brings you shame
***shameful** behaviour*

shampoo liquid soap used for washing hair

shamrock a small green plant with each leaf like three small leaves joined together

shape the pattern that a line drawn round the outside of something makes. A ball has a round shape.

share 1 to make something into parts and give them out to other people
*She **shared** out the cake.*
2 to use something that someone else is also using
*Can I **share** your book?*

shark a large sea fish with sharp teeth

sharp 1 with an edge or point that can cut or make holes

a **sharp** knife
2 sudden
a **sharp** bend in the road
3 quick to notice things or learn
sharp eyes, a **sharp** boy

shatter to break suddenly into tiny pieces

shave to cut hair from the skin to make it smooth. Men shave their faces

shawl a piece of cloth or knitting worn round the shoulders or wrapped round a baby

sheaf a bundle of corn stalks tied together at harvest time
three **sheaves**

shears a tool like a very large pair of scissors for cutting plants or for clipping wool from sheep

sheath a cover for the sharp blade of a sword or knife

sheaves more than one **sheaf**

shed **1** a small hut
2 to let something fall. Trees shed leaves, people shed tears, and caterpillars shed their skins.

sheep an animal kept by farmers for its wool and meat
two **sheep**

sheer very steep because it is straight up and down like a wall
a **sheer** cliff

sheet **1** one of the large pieces of cloth put on a bed
2 a whole piece of paper, glass, or metal

shelf a long piece of wood fastened to a wall, for putting things on
two **shelves**

shell **1** the thin, hard part round an egg, a nut, and some kinds of animals, such as snails
2 a very large bullet that explodes when it hits something

shelter a place that protects people from wind, rain, cold, or danger
a bus **shelter**

shelves more than one **shelf**

shepherd someone whose job is to look after sheep

sheriff a man in charge of the law in a county or district

shield a large piece of metal, leather, or wood used for protecting someone. Soldiers long ago held shields in front of themselves while they were fighting.

shift to move something

shimmer to shine with a light that comes and goes, like the light of the sun on water

shin the front of the leg between the knee and ankle

shine 1 to give out light
2 to look very bright
*He polished it until it **shone**.*

shingle a lot of small stones by the edge of the sea

shiny with a surface that shines

ship a large boat that takes people or things on long journeys over the sea

shipwreck a bad accident that destroys or sinks a ship while it is at sea

shirk to get out of doing something that you ought to do

shirt a piece of clothing for the top half of the body with sleeves, a collar, and buttons down the front

shiver to shake because you are cold or frightened

shoal a large number of fish swimming together

shock a big surprise that is not pleasant

shoe a strong covering for the foot, with a stiff sole and heel
*leather **shoes***

shone see **shine**

shook see **shake**

shoot 1 to use a gun or a bow and arrow
2 to hurt or kill by shooting
*A sheriff **shot** Billy the Kid.*
3 to move very quickly
4 to kick, hit, or throw a ball at the goal

shop 1 a place that people go into to buy things

2 to go to a shop to buy something

shore the land along the edge of the sea

short **1** not long
*a **short** visit*
2 not tall
*a **short** person*

shorthand a set of signs for writing words down as quickly as people say them

shorts trousers that only cover the top part of the legs

shot **1** see **shoot**
2 the firing of a gun

should ought to
*You **should** be working.*

shoulder the part of the body between the neck and arm

shout to speak very loudly

shove to push hard

shovel a kind of curved spade for lifting things such as coal or sand

show **1** to let something be seen
***Show** me your new bike.*
2 to make something clear to someone
*He's **shown** me how to do it.*
3 singing, dancing, and acting done to entertain people

4 things that have been put together and arranged so that people can come and look at them
*a flower **show***

shower **1** a short fall of rain or snow
2 a lot of small things falling like rain
*a **shower** of stones*
3 ***to have a shower*** to stand under a spray of water and wash yourself

shown see **show**

shrank see **shrink**

shred a tiny strip or piece that has been cut, broken, or torn off something

shriek a short scream

shrill sounding very high and loud
*a **shrill** whistle*

shrimp a small sea creature with a shell

shrink to become smaller
*It **shrank** when it was washed.*
*These jeans have **shrunk**.*

shrivel to get very dry and curl up at the edges like a dead leaf

shrub a bush

shrunk see **shrink**

shudder to shake suddenly because you are very cold or frightened

shuffle to drag your feet along the ground as you walk

shunt to move a train on to a different line

shut to move a cover, lid, or door in order to block up an opening
*He **shut** the door and drove off.*

shutter 1 a wooden cover that fits over a window
2 the part inside a camera that opens to let in light as you take a photograph

shy 1 not willing to meet other people because you are afraid
2 easily frightened
*a **shy** animal*

sick 1 ill
2 **to be sick** to bring food back up from the stomach through the mouth

sickening very annoying
*How **sickening**!*

side 1 one of the outer parts between the front and back of a person, animal, or thing
2 a flat surface
*A cube has six **sides**.*
3 an edge

*A triangle has three **sides**.*
4 a group playing or fighting against another group

sideboard a long, heavy piece of furniture with drawers, cupboards, and a flat top where things can be put

sideways 1 with the side first
2 to one side

siege (*say* seej) a time when the enemy surrounds a town or castle so that people and things cannot get in or out

sigh to breathe out heavily to show you are feeling very sad or very happy

sight 1 the ability to see
2 something that is seen

sign 1 anything written, drawn, or done to tell or show people something
*road **signs***
2 to write your name in your own writing

signal a sound or movement that tells people something when it is not possible to speak or shout

signature your name written by yourself in your own writing

silence a time when there is no sound at all

silent without any sound

silk very fine, shiny cloth made from threads spun by insects called **silk-worms**

sill a ledge underneath a window

silly not clever or careful
*a **silly** person, a **silly** idea*

silver a valuable, shiny white metal

similar like another person or thing
*Your dress is **similar** to mine.*

simple **1** easy
*a **simple** question*
2 plain
*a **simple** dress*
3 not complicated

since **1** from that time
2 because

sincere truly meant
***sincere** good wishes*

sing to use the voice to make a tune with sounds or words
*We have **sung** this before.*
*She **sang** a solo yesterday.*

singe to burn something slightly

single **1** only one
2 not married

sink **1** a place with taps where you do the washing-up
2 to go under water
*The ship **sank** last night.*
*It has **sunk**.*
3 to go down

sip to drink a very small amount at a time

sir **1** a word used when speaking politely to a man, instead of his name
2 a title given to knights
***Sir** Winston Churchill*

siren a machine that makes a loud sound like a scream to warn people about something

sister a girl or woman who has the same parents as another person

sit to rest on your bottom, as you do when you are on a chair
*She **sat** on the chair and broke it.*
*Are you **sitting** comfortably?*

site the ground where something has been built or will be built

situation **1** the place where something is
2 the things that are happening to you

size **1** how big something is **2** the measurement something is made in
size ten shoes

sizzle to make the noise sausages make when they are being fried

skate **1** a steel blade joined to the sole of a boot and used for moving smoothly over ice
2 to move smoothly over ice or the ground wearing skates or roller-skates

skateboard a long piece of wood or plastic on wheels. You balance on it with both feet while it moves quickly over the ground.

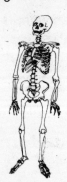

skeleton the framework of bones inside the body

sketch to draw quickly

ski a long piece of wood, metal, or plastic strapped to the foot for moving quickly and smoothly over snow
a pair of **skis**

skid to slide without meaning to

skill the ability to do something very well

skim **1** to take the cream off the top of milk
2 to move quickly over the surface of something and only just touch it

skin **1** the outer covering of the body
2 the outer covering of some fruits and vegetables

skip **1** to move lightly and quickly by hopping from one foot to the other
2 to jump over a rope that is turning
3 to miss out
Skip the next page.

skipper the person in charge of a ship or a team

skirt a piece of clothing for women and girls that hangs down from the waist

skittle one of a set of pieces of wood or plastic shaped like bottles that people try to knock down with a ball

skull the bony framework inside the head

sky the space overhead where the sun, moon, and stars can be seen

skylark a small, brown bird that sings while flying high in the air

skyscraper a very tall, modern building

slab a flat, thick piece
*a **slab** of toffee*

slack **1** not pulled tight
*a **slack** rope*
2 careless
***slack** work*
3 not busy
*a **slack** day*

slain see ***slay***

slam to close something loudly

slanting in a line that is higher at one end than the other, like the side of a triangle or a hill

slap to hit with the flat part of your hand

slash to make long cuts in something

slate one of the thin pieces of smooth, grey rock used to cover a roof

slaughter (*say* slor-ter) the killing of many people or animals

slave someone who belongs to another person and has to work without wages

slay to kill
*The dragon was **slain**.*
*St George **slew** the dragon.*

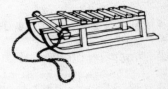

sled, sledge something used for travelling over snow with strips of metal or wood instead of wheels

sleek neat, smooth, and shiny
***sleek** hair*

sleep to close your eyes and rest completely, as you do every night.
*I **slept** in a tent last night.*

sleet a mixture of rain and snow

sleeve the part of a coat, shirt, blouse, or jersey that covers the arm

sleigh (*rhymes with* play) something used for travelling over snow. Sleighs are pulled by animals and have strips of wood or metal instead of wheels.

slender thin
*a **slender** girl*

slept see **sleep**

slew see **slay**

slide   **1** to move very quickly and smoothly over something
2 very slippery ground or a long, sloping piece of shiny metal that people can slide on
3 something pretty that girls put in their hair to keep it tidy
4 a small photograph that can be shown on a screen

slight   **1** small
a **slight** cold
2 thin
a very **slight** person

slim   **1** thin
a **slim** person
2 to try to get thinner by eating less
My sister is **slimming**.

slime wet, slippery stuff that is not pleasant

sling   **1** a piece of cloth

wrapped round an injured arm and tied round the neck so that it supports the arm

2 a short leather strap used for throwing stones

slink to move in a secret way because you are afraid or feel guilty about something
The dog saw me and **slunk** away.

slip   **1** to slide without meaning to
2 to fall over
3 to go away quickly and quietly

slipper a soft, comfortable kind of shoe worn indoors

slippery with a very smooth surface so that it is difficult to get hold of or walk on

slit a long cut or narrow opening in something

slop to make a mess by letting liquid run over the edge of a container

slope 1 ground that is like the side of a hill
2 to be slanting

slot a narrow opening for something like a coin to fit into

slouch to move, sit, or stand with the head and shoulders bent forwards

slow 1 taking more time than usual
*a **slow** train*
2 showing a time that is earlier than the correct time. Watches and clocks are sometimes slow.

sludge thick, sticky mud

slug a small creature like a snail without its shell

slumber sleep

slunk see **slink**

slush melting snow

sly clever at tricking people secretly

smack to hit with the flat part of the hand

small little
*a **small** dog*

smart 1 dressed well
2 neat and tidy
3 clever
4 to feel a stinging pain

smash to break into pieces with a loud noise

smear 1 to make a dirty mark by rubbing against something
2 to rub something over a surface

smell 1 to use the nose to find out about something
*I bent down and **smelt** the rose.*
2 anything that can be smelt

smile to make your face show that you are happy

smith someone who makes things out of metal

smock a very loose dress or blouse

smoke 1 blue or grey gas that floats up from a fire and looks like a cloud
2 to have a cigarette or pipe between the lips, take in the smoke from it, and breathe it out

smooth free from lumps or rough parts
*a **smooth** surface*

smother 1 to cover thickly
*a cake **smothered** in cream*
2 to cover someone's mouth and nose so that he cannot breathe

smoulder to burn slowly with a lot of smoke

smudge a dirty mark made by rubbing against something

smuggle to bring something into a country secretly without paying the tax that should be paid to the government

snack something you can eat quickly instead of a meal

snail a small creature that lives inside a shell. Snails are found on land and in water.

snake a creature with a long body and no legs. Some snakes can give poisonous bites.

snap **1** to break something suddenly by bending or stretching it
2 to bite suddenly

snapshot a photograph

snare a trap for catching animals

snarl to make the sound a dog makes when it is angry

snatch to take something quickly

sneak **1** someone who tells tales

2 to move, trying not to be seen or heard

sneer to speak or smile in an insulting way that shows that you think someone is not worth bothering about

sneeze to make a sudden noise as air rushes out of the nose
*I can't stop **sneezing**.*

sniff to make a noise by suddenly taking in air through the nose

snip to cut a little bit off something

snob someone who only bothers with people that he thinks are clever or important

snooker a game played on a long table with rods and twenty-two small, coloured balls

snore to breathe very noisily while sleeping

snorkel

snorkel a tube for someone to breathe through while he is swimming under water

snout an animal's nose and mouth sticking out from the rest of its face. Pigs have snouts.

snow small, thin, white pieces of frozen water. Snow floats down from the sky when the weather is very cold.

snowdrop a small white flower that grows in January and February

snub to show someone who is trying to be friendly that you do not want to be his friend

snug cosy

snuggle to curl up in a warm comfortable place

soak to make something very wet

soap something used with water for washing

soar to move high into the air

sock a covering for the foot and part of the leg

socket the part that an electric light bulb or plug fits into

sofa a long, comfortable seat with a back, for more than one person

soft **1** not firm. Cotton wool and wet clay are soft. **2** not loud

soggy wet through

soil the brown stuff on the ground, that plants grow in

solar having to do with the sun
*the **solar** system*

sold see **sell**

soldier a member of the army

sole **1** the flat part underneath a foot or shoe **2** a sea fish that is eaten

solemn serious
*a **solemn** face*

solid **1** not hollow **2** firm. Liquids and gases are not solid.
__solid__ food

solitary alone or lonely

solo something sung, played, danced, or done by one person

solution the answer to a puzzle or problem

solve to find the answer to a puzzle

some **1** a few
__some__ sweets
2 a certain amount of
__some__ cake

3 a, an, or one
some animal

somebody a person

somehow in some way

someone a person

somersault (*say* summer-solt)
1 a jump, turning head over heels in the air
2 a forward or backward roll on the ground

something some thing

sometimes at some times

somewhere in some place or to some place

son a boy or man who is someone's child

song words that are sung

soon in a very short time from now

soot the black powder left behind by smoke

soothe to make someone who is upset feel calm
soothing words

sorcerer a man in fairy tales, who can do magic things

sore painful when it is touched
sore skin

sorrow a very sad feeling

sorry **1** sad about something that you wish you had not done
2 sad because of something that has happened to another person

sort **1** a kind
I like this sort best.
2 to arrange things into different groups

sought see **seek**

soul the part of a person that cannot be seen but is believed to go on living after he has died

sound **1** anything that can be heard
2 to make a sound

soup a hot liquid made from meat or vegetables

sour **1** with the kind of taste lemons and vinegar have
2 not fresh
sour milk

source the place something has come from

south the direction to your right when you face east

southern from the south or in the south

souvenir (*say* soo-ven-eer) something that you keep because it makes you think about a person or place

sovereign a ruler who is a king, queen, emperor, or empress

sow[1] (*rhymes with* toe) to put seeds in the ground so that they will grow into plants *The grain was* **sown** *in the spring.*

sow[2] (*rhymes with* how) a female pig

space **1** the distance between things **2** a place with nothing in it **3** all the places beyond the earth, where the stars and planets are. Outer space is so vast that it cannot be measured.

spaceship a machine that can carry people and things through space

spade **1** a tool with a long handle and a short, wide blade for digging **2** a small, black spade printed on some playing-cards

spaghetti a food that looks like long pieces of string when it is cooked

span **1** to reach from one side of something to the other, as a bridge does **2** the distance between the top of the thumb and the top of the little finger when the hand is spread out

spaniel a kind of dog with silky fur and long ears

spank to hit someone hard on the bottom

spanner a tool that fits round a nut so that you can turn it to make it tighter or looser

spare **1** not used but kept in case it is needed *a* **spare** *tyre* **2** to give up something so that someone else can have it

spark **1** a tiny piece of burning stuff **2** a tiny flash

sparkle to shine with a lot of tiny flashes of bright light *sparkling jewels*

sparkler a kind of firework that sparkles. You can hold it in your hand while it burns.

195

sparrow a small, brown bird that is often seen in gardens

spat see **spit**

spawn the eggs of frogs, fish, and some other creatures

speak to say something
*She **spoke** to me yesterday.
I've not **spoken** to him yet.*

spear a long pole or stick with a very sharp point, used as a weapon

special   **1** different from any other kind
2 for one person or thing
*a **special** cake for my birthday*

specimen   **1** a small amount of something that shows what the rest is like
2 an example of one kind of plant or animal

speck   **1** a tiny mark
2 a tiny bit of dust

speckled with small, coloured spots. Some birds' eggs are speckled.

spectacles a pair of glasses

spectator someone watching a game or show

speech   **1** the power of speaking
2 a talk given to a group of people

speed how quickly something moves or happens

spell   **1** to write a word correctly
*How is your name **spelt**?*
2 magic words that make things happen

spend   **1** to use money to pay for things
2 to pass time
*I **spent** yesterday at home.*

sphere (*say* sfear)
the shape of a ball (see the list of shapes on page 249)

spice part of a plant such as the berry or seed that is dried and used in cooking to give food a stronger flavour. Ginger and pepper are spices.

spider a small creature with eight legs that sometimes weaves webs to catch insects

spike a thin piece of metal with a sharp point

spill to let something fall out of a container
*The cat drank the **spilt** milk.*

spin   **1** to turn round and round quickly
*I **spun** round until I was dizzy.*
2 to make thread by twisting

long, thin pieces of wool or cotton together

spinach (*say* spin-itch) a vegetable with a lot of green leaves, eaten cooked

spine **1** the long bone down the centre of the back **2** a thorn or prickle

spinning-wheel a machine for spinning thread. It is worked by the hand or foot.

spinster a woman who has not married

spiral **1** the shape of a line that keeps going round the same point in smaller and smaller or bigger and bigger curves, like the jam in a slice of Swiss roll (see the list of shapes on pages 248–9) **2** *a spiral staircase* a staircase that you go round and round as you climb up it

spire a tall, pointed part on top of a church tower

spirit **1** the part of a person that cannot be seen but is believed to go on living after he has died **2** a ghost **3** something that makes a person very brave and lively

spit to send drops of liquid out of the mouth *The cat **spat** when it saw the dog.*

spiteful full of a wish to hurt someone by what you say or do

splash **1** to make drops of water fly about as they do when you jump into water **2** the noise you make when you jump into water

splendid **1** very good *a **splendid** holiday* **2** looking very grand *a **splendid** uniform*

splint a straight piece of wood or metal that is tied to a broken arm or leg to hold it firm

splinter a sharp bit of wood, glass, or metal

split to break something into parts
*He **split** the log with an axe.*

spoil **1** to make something less good or useful than it was
2 to be too kind to a child so that he thinks he can always have what he wants
*The little boy was very **spoilt**.*

spoke **1** see **speak**
2 one of the wires or rods that go from the centre of a wheel to the rim

spoken see **speak**

sponge **1** a light, soft cake
2 something thick and soft with a lot of holes in it. Sponges soak up water and are used for washing.

spool a round piece of wood or metal that cotton, string, or film is wound on

spoon the tool you use for eating soup and pudding

sport a game or something else that is usually done outside and exercises the body. Running, jumping, football, and netball are all sports.

spot **1** a round mark
2 a small, round swelling on the skin
3 a place
4 to notice something
*She **spotted** the mistake at once.*

spotlight a strong light that can shine on one small area

spout the part of a container that is made like a pipe so that you can pour liquid out of it easily. Teapots and kettles have spouts.

sprain to twist the wrist or ankle so that it swells and is painful

sprang see **spring**

sprawl to sit or lie with your arms and legs spread out

spray to make tiny drops of liquid fall all over something

spread **1** to stretch something out to its full size
*The bird **spread** its wings.*
2 to make something cover a surface

spring **1** the part of the year when plants start to grow

and the days are getting lighter and warmer
2 a place where water comes out of the ground
3 a piece of metal wound into rings so that it jumps back into shape after it has been pressed or stretched
4 to move suddenly upwards
*I **sprang** up and caught the ball.*
*Weeds had **sprung** up everywhere.*

sprinkle to make a few tiny pieces or drops fall on something

sprint to run a short distance very quickly

sprout   **1** to start to grow
*The seeds soon **sprouted**.*
2 a vegetable that looks like a tiny cabbage
*Brussels **sprouts***

sprung see **spring**

spun see **spin**

spurt   **1** to move like water shooting suddenly upwards
2 to get suddenly faster near the end of a race

spy   **1** someone who works secretly to find out things about another person or country
2 to notice
*I **spy** with my little eye . . .*

3 to be a spy

squabble to quarrel about something that is not important

square a flat shape with four straight sides that are all the same length (see the list of shapes on page 248)

squash   **1** to press something hard so that it goes out of shape
2 a drink made from fruit
3 a game played indoors with rackets and a small rubber ball

squat to sit on the ground with your knees bent and your bottom resting on your heels

squaw a female American Indian

squeak to make the tiny, shrill sound a mouse makes

squeal to make a long, shrill sound

squeeze to press something between your hands or two other things

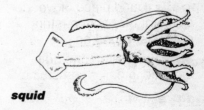

squid

199

squid a sea creature with eight short arms and two very long ones

squirm to twist and turn the body about, like a worm

squirrel a small animal with a very thick tail that lives in trees

squirt to make a thin stream of liquid come suddenly out of something

stab to hit someone with the sharp, pointed end of a knife or sword

stable a building in which horses are kept

stack a neat pile

stadium a large place where people can watch sports and games

staff 1 a group of people who work together in an office, shop, or school
2 a thick stick for walking with

stag a male deer

stage 1 a raised floor in a hall or theatre, on which people act, sing, or dance to entertain other people
2 the point someone has reached in doing something

stagger to try to stand or walk but find it difficult to stay upright

stagnant not flowing or fresh
*a pool of **stagnant** water*

stain a dirty mark made on something

stair one of a set of steps for going up or down inside a building

staircase a set of stairs and banisters

stake a thick, pointed stick

stale not fresh
stale bread

stalk 1 a thin stem
2 to walk in a stiff way that shows you are angry
3 to move secretly to get close to an animal you are hunting

stall 1 a kind of small shop or a table that things are sold on. Markets have stalls.
2 a place for one animal in a stable or shed

stallion a male horse

stammer to keep repeating the sounds at the beginning of words when you speak

stamp 1 to bang the foot heavily on the ground
2 a piece of sticky paper with a picture on it. People

put stamps on letters and parcels to show that they have paid to post them.

stand **1** to be on your feet without moving
I **stood** there until they came.
2 something made for putting things on
a cake **stand**, a hat **stand**

standard **1** how good something is
a high **standard** of work
2 a flag

stank see **stink**

star **1** one of the tiny, bright lights you see in the sky at night
2 a famous singer or actor

starch a powder or liquid for making clothes stiff

stare to look at someone or something for a long time, without moving your eyes

starling a dark brown bird often seen in large flocks

start **1** to take the first steps in doing something
2 to make something happen

startle to make a person or animal very surprised and frightened
startling news

starvation illness or death caused by great hunger

starve to be very ill or die because you have not got enough food

state **1** how someone or something is
2 to say something important
3 a country or part of a country
United **States** of America

statement words that say something important

station **1** a place where people get on or off trains
2 a building for policemen or firemen

statue a model of a person made in stone or metal

stay **1** to be in the same place
2 to live somewhere as a visitor

steady not shaking in any way
a **steady** voice, a **steady** hand

steak (rhymes with rake) a thick slice of meat or fish

steal to take something that does not belong to you and keep it
A dog **stole** the meat yesterday.

*The jewels were **stolen**.*

steam very hot water that has turned into a gas that cannot be seen

steel a strong, shiny metal made from iron

steep sloping sharply
*a **steep** hill*

steeple a tall, pointed tower on top of a church

steer 1 to make a ship, car, or bicycle go in the direction you want
2 a young bull kept for its meat

stem 1 the main part of a plant above the ground
2 the thin part that joins a leaf, flower, or fruit to the rest of the plant

step 1 the movement you make with your foot when you are walking, running, or dancing
2 a flat place where you can put your foot when you are going up or down something

stepfather a man who is married to your mother but is not your real father

stepmother a woman who is married to your father but is not your real mother

stern 1 the back end

of a boat
2 severe or strict

stew 1 meat and vegetables cooked in liquid
2 to cook something slowly in liquid

stick 1 a long, thin piece of wood
2 a long, thin piece of anything
*a **stick** of liquorice*
3 to become fastened or joined to things, as glue and mud do
*The sweets were **stuck** to the bag.*
4 to press a sharp point into something

sticky able to stick things. Glue, jam, and honey are all sticky.

stiff not easily bent
stiff cardboard

stile a set of steps made to help people to get over a fence

still 1 not moving
*Hold it **still**.*
2 the same now as before
*He is **still** ill.*

stilts a pair of poles with which you can walk high above the ground

sting 1 a sharp part with poison on it that some

stilts

animals and plants have
2 to hurt someone with a
sting
A bee **stung** *me yesterday.*

stink to have a very strong,
bad smell
The stable was filthy and
stank.
It has always **stunk** *like*
this.

stir **1** to move a liquid or a
soft mixture round with a
spoon
2 to start to move

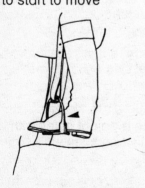

stirrup the metal part that

hangs down each side of a
horse's saddle for you to put
your foot in while you are
riding

stitch **1** a loop of thread
made by the needle in
sewing
2 one of the loops of wool on
a knitting needle
3 a sudden pain in the side.
People sometimes get
stitches when they have
been running.

stoat a small, brown, furry
animal with a long body that
kills and eats mice, rats,
birds, and rabbits

stock **1** a lot of things kept
ready to be sold or used
2 a garden flower with a
sweet smell

stocking a covering for the
foot and leg worn next to the
skin

stoke to put coal or wood on a
fire to keep it burning

stole, stolen see **steal**

stomach the part in the
middle of the body, where
food goes when it is eaten

stone **1** rock
2 a small piece of rock
3 the hard seed in the middle
of a cherry, plum, peach, or
apricot

203

4 a measure for weight
*She weighs 4 **stone**.*

stood see **stand**

stool a small seat without a back

stoop to bend the body forwards

stop **1** to end
2 to come to rest
*The bus **stopped**.*
3 to stay

stopper something that fits into the top of a bottle to close it

store **1** to keep things until they are needed
2 a large shop

storey all the rooms on the same floor in a building

stork a large bird with very long legs and a long beak

storm a very strong wind with a lot of rain or snow

story words that tell you about something that has really happened or about something that someone has made up
*adventure **stories***

stout fat
*a **stout** lady*

stove something that gives out heat for warming a room or for cooking

straight **1** like a line drawn with a ruler
*a **straight** road*
2 **straight away** at once

straighten **1** to make something straight
2 to become straight

strain **1** to stretch, push, or try too hard
2 to hurt part of yourself by stretching or pushing too hard
3 to separate a liquid from lumps or other things floating in it. People strain tea to get rid of the tea leaves.

strange **1** not known or seen before
*a **strange** place*
2 unusual and very surprising
*a **strange** story*

stranger **1** someone in a place he does not know
2 someone you do not know

strangle to kill someone by pressing on his throat until he cannot breathe

strap a flat strip of leather or another strong material for fastening things together

straw **1** dry stalks of corn
2 a very thin tube for drinking through

strawberry a small, red, juicy fruit
strawberry *jam*

stray lost and without a home
a **stray** *cat*

streak **1** a long, narrow mark
2 to move very quickly

stream water that is moving along in one direction

streamer a long strip of paper or a ribbon joined by one end to something to decorate it

street a road with buildings along each side

strength how strong someone or something is

stretch to pull something to make it longer, wider, or tighter

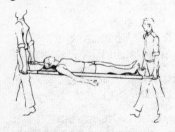

stretcher a pair of poles with canvas stretched across them for carrying a sick or injured person

strict keen on always being obeyed

strict parents

stride to walk with long steps
I **strode** *angrily out of the room.*

strike **1** to hit
The house was **struck** *by lightning.*
2 *to strike a match* to rub a match along something rough so that it bursts into flame
3 to stop working until the people in charge agree to make things better

string very thin rope

strip **1** a long, narrow piece
2 to take off clothes or a covering

stripe a coloured band across or down something

strode see **stride**

stroke **1** to move the hand gently along something
2 a hitting movement

stroll to walk slowly, because you are enjoying your walk and do not have to get anywhere

strong **1** healthy and able to do things that need a lot of energy
a **strong** *horse*
2 not easily broken
strong rope

3 with a lot of flavour
strong tea

struck see **strike**

structure **1** anything that
has been built
2 the way something has
been built

struggle **1** to use your arms
and legs in fighting or trying
to get free
2 to try very hard to do
something you find difficult

stubborn not willing to
change your ideas even
though they might be
wrong

stuck see **stick**

stud a small knob like the
ones on the sole of a football
boot

student someone who studies
at college or university

studio a place where films or
radio or television
programmes are made

study **1** to spend time
learning about something
2 to look at something very
carefully
3 a room where someone
studies

stuff **1** anything used for
making things
2 to fill something tightly

3 to push something inside
another thing

stuffy without fresh air
a *stuffy* room

stumble to fall over
something

stump **1** the part of a broken
tree, tooth, or pencil that is
left
2 one of the set of three
upright sticks put at each
end of the pitch in cricket
(see **wicket**)

stun **1** to hit or hurt someone
so much that he cannot think
properly
2 to make someone very
surprised

stung see **sting**

stunk see **stink**

stupid **1** very silly
a *stupid* idea
2 slow to learn and
understand

sturdy strong and healthy
a *sturdy* child

stutter to keep repeating the
sounds at the beginning of
words when you speak

sty **1** a sore swelling on the
edge of an eyelid
2 a place where pigs are
kept
two *sties*

style the way something is done or made

subject **1** the person or thing that you are writing about or learning about
2 someone who is ruled by a king, queen, or government

submarine a ship that can travel under water

substance anything that can be seen, touched, or used for making things

subtract to find the answer to a sum like this $6 - 3 =$

subway a tunnel made under the ground so that people can get to the other side of a road safely

succeed to do or get what you wanted to do or get

successful able to do or get what you wanted to do or get

such **1** of the same kind
sweets **such** as these
2 so great
It was **such** a surprise!

suck **1** to take in air or liquid from something
I **sucked** milk through a straw.
2 to keep moving something around inside your mouth without chewing it
He **sucked** a sweet.

sudden happening quickly without any warning
a **sudden** scream

suede (say swade)
a kind of soft leather that is not shiny

suet (say soo-it)
hard fat that comes from sheep and cattle and is used in cooking

suffer to have to put up with pain or something else that is not pleasant

sufficient enough

sugar a sweet food that is put in drinks and other foods to make them taste sweet

suggest to give someone an idea that you think is useful

suit **1** a jacket and a pair of trousers or skirt that are meant to be worn together
2 to fit in with someone's plans
3 to look well on someone
That colour **suits** you.

suitable just right for

something
suitable *shoes for dancing*

suitcase a kind of box with a lid and a handle for carrying clothes and other things on journeys

suite (*say* sweet) a set of furniture

sulk to stop speaking to your friends, because you are angry about something

sultana a dried grape

summer the hottest part of the year

summit the top of a mountain

sun the large, round light in the sky that gives the earth heat and light

sundial a kind of clock that uses a shadow made by the sun to show what time it is

sung see **sing**

sunk see **sink**

sunny with the sun shining
*a **sunny** day*

sunrise the time when the sun rises

sunset the time when the sun goes down

sunshine the light and heat that come from the sun when it is shining

supermarket a large shop where people help themselves to things as they go round and pay for them all on the way out

supersonic faster than sound travels
*a **supersonic** aeroplane*

supper a meal or snack eaten in the evening

supply **1** to give what is needed
2 things kept ready to be used when needed
*a **supply** of paper*

support **1** to hold up something so that it does not fall
2 to give help to someone

suppose to think something is true although it might not be

sure knowing something is true or right
*I'm **sure** I'm right.*

surface 1 the part all round the outside of something 2 the top of a table or desk

surgeon a doctor who is trained to do operations

surgery the room you go in to see a doctor or dentist

surname your last name that is the same as your family's name

surprise 1 the feeling you have when something suddenly happens that you were not expecting 2 something that happens and was not expected

surrender to stop fighting and agree to obey the enemy

surround to be all round someone or something

suspect to have a feeling that there might be something wrong

suspicious feeling that there might be something wrong a **suspicious** policeman

swallow 1 to make something go down your throat 2 a bird with a dark blue body, a long tail, and pointed wings

swam see **swim**

swamp an area of very wet ground

swan a big white bird with a very long neck that lives on water or near to it

swap (rhymes with hop) to change one thing for another thing

swarm a large number of insects together a **swarm** of bees

sway to move from side to side

swear 1 to make a very serious promise He has **sworn** to tell the truth. 2 to use bad words He **swore** when he hit his finger.

sweat to lose liquid through your skin, because you are ill or very hot

sweater a jersey

sweep 1 to use a brush to clear away dust and litter from something I **swept** this floor yesterday. 2 someone whose job is to clean chimneys

sweet 1 with the taste of sugar or honey 2 very pleasant

a **sweet** *smell*
3 a small piece of sweet
food made of sugar or
chocolate
a bag of **sweets**
4 a pudding

swell to get bigger
My broken ankle has
swollen.

swelling a swollen place on
the body

swept see **sweep**

swerve to move suddenly to
one side so that you will not
bump into something

swift **1** quick
2 a bird with long wings that
flies very quickly

swill the food and liquid given
to pigs

swim **1** to move the body
through water, without
touching the bottom
I **swam** *a length yesterday.*
2 to cross water by
swimming
She has **swum** *the
Channel.*

swindle to make someone
believe something that is not
true in order to get something
valuable from him

swing **1** to move backwards
and forwards, from side to
side, or in a curve

The door **swung** *open
in the wind.*
2 a seat hung from a tree
or metal bar so that it can
move backwards and
forwards

swipe to hit hard

swirl to move around quickly
in circles

switch **1** anything that is
turned or pressed in order to
make something work or stop
working
an electric light **switch**
2 to change from one thing
to another

swollen see **swell**

swoop to fly down suddenly to
attack something

sword (*say* sord)
a weapon like a knife with a
very long blade

swore, sworn see **swear**

swum see **swim**

swung see **swing**

sycamore a kind of large
tree. Its seeds have wings
and so they can be carried a
long way by the wind.

syllable (*say* silabul)
any word or part of a word
that has one separate sound
when you say it. *Bi-cy-cle*

has three syllables and *bike* has one syllable.

symmetrical with two halves that are exactly alike but the opposite way round. Butterflies, spectacles, and wheels are symmetrical. (See page 249)

sympathy the feeling you have when you are sorry for someone who is sad, ill, or in trouble, and want to help him

syrup a very sweet, sticky liquid

system a set of parts, things, or ideas that work together

Tt

tabby **1** a grey or brown cat with dark stripes in its fur
2 a female cat

table **1** a piece of furniture with a flat top and legs
2 a list of facts arranged in order

table-cloth a piece of material spread over a table to cover it

tablet a small, solid piece of medicine

tack **1** a short nail with a flat top
2 to sew two pieces of material together quickly, with long stitches

tackle **1** to try to do a job that needs doing
2 to try to get the ball from someone else in a football game
3 all the things needed for doing something
fishing **tackle**

tadpole a tiny creature that lives in water and will turn into a frog or toad

tail the part at the end of something. Most animals have tails and so do aeroplanes.

tailor someone whose job is to make suits and coats

take **1** to get hold of something
He **took** *his prize and smiled.*
2 to carry or lead away
The money was **taken** *yesterday.*
Dad is **taking** *us to the zoo.*

tale a story

talent the ability to do

something very well
a **talent** *for singing*

talk to speak to other people

talkative fond of talking

tall measuring more than usual from top to bottom
a **tall** *person, a* **tall** *tree*

tambourine a musical instrument that you shake or hit with your fingers

tame not wild or dangerous. Tame animals can be kept as pets, because they are not frightened of people.

tamper to make changes in something so that it will not work properly
I **tampered** *with the car so that it would not start.*

tan **1** skin that has gone brown because of the sun
2 light brown
3 to make the skin of an animal into leather

tangerine a kind of small orange

tangled twisted up in knots
tangled *wool,* **tangled** *hair*

tank **1** a large container for liquid. Fish tanks are made of glass and hot water tanks are made of metal.

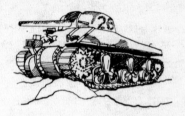

2 a kind of very strong, heavy car used in war. It has a big gun on top and two long strips of metal round its wheels so that it can move over rough ground.

tanker **1** a large ship for carrying oil

2 a large lorry for carrying milk or petrol

tape **1** a narrow strip of cotton used in tying things and making loops or labels for clothes
2 a narrow strip of special

plastic used in a tape-recorder

taper **1** a kind of very thin candle used for lighting fires **2** to get very narrow at one end

tape-recorder a machine that can take sound down on special tape or make sound come out of a tape

tapestry a piece of strong cloth covered with stitches that make a picture

tar a thick, black, sticky liquid made from coal or wood and used for making roads

target something that people aim at and try to hit

tart **1** pastry with jam or fruit on it **2** very sour. Rhubarb without sugar tastes tart.

tartan Scottish woollen cloth woven with a check pattern and used for making kilts

task a piece of work that must be done

tassel a bundle of threads tied together at the top and used to decorate things

taste **1** to eat a little bit of food or sip a drink to see what it is like

2 the flavour something has when you taste it

tasty with a strong, pleasant taste
tasty kippers

tattered badly torn

taught see **teach**

tax money that people have to give to the government

taxi a car that you can travel in if you pay the driver
two **taxis**

tea **1** a hot drink made with boiling water and the dried leaves of a **tea-plant** **2** a meal eaten in the afternoon

teach to make someone else able to understand or do something
She **taught** me to swim last year.

teacher someone whose job is to teach

team a group of people who work together or play together on the same side in a game

teapot a kind of jug with a spout and lid, used for making tea

tear[1] (*rhymes with* fear) a small drop of water that

comes out of the eye when you cry

tear [2] (*rhymes with* fair)
to pull something apart so that you damage it
I **tore** *the letter up and threw it away.*
His coat was **torn**.

tease to bother or annoy someone for fun
Stop **teasing** *her!*

teem **1** to rain very hard
2 to be full of moving things
The river was **teeming** *with fish.*

teenager someone who is between thirteen and nineteen years old

teeth more than one **tooth**

telegram a short message that the post office sends very quickly along electric wires

telegraph **1** to send a telegram
2 telegraph pole a tall pole that holds up telephone wires

telephone **1** an instrument that makes sound travel along wires so that you can use it to speak to someone far away
2 to use a telephone to speak to someone

telescope a tube with lenses at each end. People look through telescopes in order to see things that are far away

television a machine that picks up programmes sent through the air and changes them into pictures and sound so that people can watch them

tell to speak in order to pass on news, a story, or instructions
I **told** *you about it yesterday.*

temper **1** the mood someone is in
in a good **temper**
in a bad **temper**
2 to lose your temper to become very angry

temperature how hot or cold something is

temple a place where

some people worship

temporary for a short time only

tempt to try to make someone do wrong

temptation something that makes you want to do wrong

tend **1** to be likely to do something
He **tends** to fall asleep after dinner.
2 to look after

tender **1** loving
a **tender** smile
2 soft
tender meat
3 sore
tender skin

tennis a game played by two or four people with rackets and a ball on a court with a net across the middle

tent a kind of shelter made of canvas stretched over poles. People sleep in tents when they are camping.

tepid only just warm
tepid water

term the time between the main holidays, when school is open. There are three school terms in a year.

terminus the place where a

bus or train stops at the end of its journey

terrace **1** a raised, flat piece of ground next to a house or in a garden
2 a row of houses that are joined together
3 one of the set of stone steps where people stand to watch football matches
the **terraces**

terrapin a creature that lives in water and looks like a small tortoise

terrible very bad
terrible weather

terrier a kind of small dog

terrific **1** very good
a **terrific** idea
2 very big
a **terrific** bang

terrify to make a person or animal very frightened

territory land that belongs to one country or person

terror great fear

test **1** questions you have to

answer to show how good you are at something
*a spelling **test***
2 to try out
***Test** the brakes.*

tether to tie an animal up so that it has room to move about, but cannot get away

than compared with another person or thing
*You are smaller **than** me.*

thank to tell someone you are pleased about something he has given you or done for you
***Thank** you for the present.*

thankful wanting to thank someone for what he has done
*She felt very **thankful**.*

that the one there
***That** is mine, this is yours.*
***Those** books are yours.*

thatch straw or reeds used for covering a roof

thaw **1** to make ice or snow melt
2 the melting of ice or snow

theatre a place where people go to see plays and shows

theft stealing
*the **theft** of the diamond*

their belonging to them
***their** coats*

them see **they**

themselves **1** they and no one else
2 *by **themselves*** on their own

then **1** after that
2 at that time
*We didn't know about it **then**.*

there in that place or to that place
*stand **there**!*

therefore and so

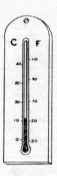

thermometer an instrument that measures temperature

these see **this**

they the people or things you are talking about
***They** all like cake.*
*I gave each of **them** a sweet.*

thick measuring a lot from one side to the other
*a **thick** slice of cake*

thicken **1** to make thicker
2 to get thicker

thief someone who steals
things
Ali Baba and the forty
thieves

thigh the top part of the leg
down to the knee

thimble a metal or plastic
cover for the end of a finger.
You wear it when you sew to
protect your finger from the
needle.

thin not fat or thick

thing anything that can be
seen or touched

think **1** to use your mind
2 to have an idea
*I **thought** you were wrong.*

third **1** one of the three equal
parts something can be
divided into. It can also be
written as $\frac{1}{3}$.
2 coming after the second
third prize

thirst the need for drink

thirsty wanting a drink

this the one here
This *is mine, that is yours.*
These *books are mine.*

thistle a wild plant with prickly
leaves and purple flowers

thorn a sharp, pointed part on
a plant's stem. Roses have
thorns.

thorough **1** done properly
and carefully
thorough work
2 complete
*a **thorough** mess*

those see **that**

though and yet or although
*It was very cold **though** it
didn't snow.*

thought **1** see **think**
2 something that you think

thoughtful **1** thinking a lot
*She looked **thoughtful**.*
2 thinking kindly about
others and what they would
like

thrash to keep hitting
someone with a stick

thread **1** a long, thin piece
of cotton, nylon, or wool
used for sewing or weaving
cloth
2 to put thread through the
eye of a needle or the hole in
a bead

threat a promise that you
will do something bad if
what you want does not
happen

threaten to make threats

thresh to get the seeds out of
corn by beating it

threw see **throw**

thrifty careful with money

thrill a sudden excited feeling

thrilling very exciting

throat the front of the neck and the tube inside it that takes foods, liquid, and air into the body

throb to beat heavily. Your heart throbs when you have been running very fast.

throne a special chair for a king or queen

throng a large number of people

throttle to kill someone by squeezing his throat until he cannot breathe

through from one end or side to the other
*We went **through** the tunnel.*

throughout all through
*It was hot **throughout** the day.*

throw to make something move through the air
*He **threw** a stone and smashed the window.*
*Jonah was **thrown** into the sea.*

thrush a bird that has a white front with brown spots on it

thrust to push hard
*He **thrust** his sword into the monster and killed it.*

thud to make the low, dull sound something heavy and large makes when it hits the ground

thumb the short, thick finger at the side of each hand

thump to hit hard with the fist

thunder the loud noise that you hear after a flash of lightning in a storm

thunderstorm a storm with thunder and lightning

tick **1** to make the sound a clock or watch keeps making when it is working
2 a small mark like this √

ticket a piece of paper or card that you buy so that you can travel on a bus or train or get into places like cinemas and theatres

tickle to keep touching part of someone's body lightly with your fingers or a feather. Most people laugh when they are tickled.

tide the movement of the sea towards the land and away from the land

tidy neatly arranged with

nothing out of place
*a **tidy** room*

tie **1** to fasten something with a knot or bow
*He's **tying** it up with ribbon.*
2 a long strip of material tied round the collar of a shirt so that the ends hang down the front

tiger a big wild cat found in India and China. It has yellow fur with black stripes.

tight fitting very closely
***tight** shoes, a **tight** lid*

tighten **1** to make tighter
2 to get tighter

tights a piece of clothing that fits closely over the feet, legs, and lower part of the body
*a pair of **tights***

tile a thin piece of baked clay or something else that is stiff, used in covering a roof, wall, or floor

till **1** until
2 a drawer or box for money in a shop

tilt to make something slope

timber wood that can be used for making things

time **1** seconds, minutes, hours, days, weeks, months, and years

2 a certain moment in the day
*What **time** is it? It's **time** for tea.*
3 the rhythm and speed of a piece of music

timid not brave

tingle to sting a little bit
*Her ears were **tingling** with the cold.*

tinkle to make the light, ringing sound a small bell makes

tinsel thin, shiny, silver ribbon. Tinsel is used for decorating things at Christmas.

tiny very small

tip **1** the part right at the end of something
2 a small gift of money given to someone for his help
3 a place where rubbish is left
4 to turn something over so that the things inside it fall out

tiptoe to walk on your toes without making a sound
*She **tiptoed** away.*

tired **1** needing to rest or sleep
2 bored with something
*I'm **tired** of work.*

tissue very thin, soft paper

title **1** the name of a book, film, picture, or piece of music
2 a word like Sir, Lady, Dr, Mr, and Mrs that is put in front of a person's name

titter to laugh in a silly way

toad an animal like a big frog. It has rough, dry skin and lives on land.

toadstool a plant that looks like a mushroom. Most toadstools are poisonous.

toast bread cooked until it is crisp and brown
beans on **toast**

tobacco a plant with leaves that are dried and smoked in pipes or used to make cigars and cigarettes

toboggan a kind of sledge used for sliding down slopes covered in snow

today this day

toddler a young child just beginning to walk

toe one of the five separate parts at the end of each foot

toffee butter and sugar cooked together and made into sticky sweets

together **1** with another
joined **together**
2 at the same time as another
They sang **together**.

toil to do hard work

toilet a lavatory

token a round piece of plastic or a kind of ticket, used instead of money to pay for something
bus **tokens**, record **tokens**

told see **tell**

tomato a soft, round, red vegetable with seeds inside it. Tomatoes are eaten raw in salads.

tomb (rhymes with room) a place where a dead person's body is buried. Some tombs are above the ground.

tomboy a girl who likes doing things that boys usually do

tomorrow the day after today

ton a large measure for weight

tone **1** a musical sound
2 the kind of sound someone's voice has
a gentle **tone**

tongs a tool that looks like a pair of scissors and is used for getting hold of something and picking it up

*a pair of sugar **tongs***

tongue the long, soft, pink part that moves about inside the mouth

tonight this evening or night

tonsils parts of the throat that sometimes cause an illness called **tonsillitis**

too **1** as well
*Can I come **too**?*
2 more than is needed
***too** much*

took see **take**

tool something that you use to help you to do a job. Hammers and saws are tools.

tooth one of the hard, white parts in the mouth
*Brush your **teeth** after every meal.*

toothache a pain in a tooth

toothbrush a small brush with a long handle, for cleaning teeth

toothpaste a thick paste put on a toothbrush and used for cleaning teeth

topic something interesting that you are writing about or talking about

topple to fall over because there is too much on top
*The pile of bricks **toppled** over.*

topsy-turvy turned upside-down

torch an electric light that you can carry about with you

tore see **tear²**

torment to keep bothering or annoying someone for fun, although it is cruel

torn see **tear²**

torpedo a kind of long, round bomb sent under water to destroy ships and submarines
*two **torpedoes***

torrent a very fast stream of water

tortoise a creature with four legs and a shell over its body, that moves slowly

torture **1** great pain that seems as if it will never end
2 to make someone feel great pain

toss to throw into the air

total the amount when you have added everything up

totter to walk very shakily as if you are going to fall over. Young children totter when they are learning to walk.

touch **1** to feel something with part of your body
*He **touched** the wet paint with his finger.*
2 to be so close to something else that there is no space in between

tough **1** strong
***tough** shoes, a **tough** fighter*
2 hard to chew
***tough** meat*

tour **1** a journey you make to visit different places
2 to walk round a place looking at different things

tow to pull along with a rope or chain
*The truck **towed** the car to a garage.*

toward, towards in the direction of something
*He walked **towards** the school.*

towel a piece of cloth for drying things that are wet
*a bath **towel**, a tea **towel***

tower **1** a tall, narrow building

*Blackpool **Tower***
2 a tall, narrow part of a building
*a church **tower***

town a place with schools, shops, offices, factories, and a lot of houses built near each other

towpath a path beside a canal or river

toy something you play with

trace **1** a mark left by something
2 to copy a picture using thin paper that you can see through. You put the paper over the picture and follow its lines with a pencil.

track **1** a kind of path
2 a railway line
3 to follow the marks left by a person or animal

tractor a machine with wheels and an engine that is used on farms to pull heavy things

trade buying and selling

traffic cars, buses, bicycles, lorries, and other things travelling on the road

tragedy **1** something very sad that has happened
2 a play with a very sad ending

trail 1 a rough path
2 smells and marks left behind by an animal. People follow trails when they are hunting.
3 to be dragged along the ground
*Your scarf is **trailing** in the mud.*

trailer something that is pulled along by a car or lorry

train 1 railway coaches joined together and pulled by an engine
2 to teach a person or animal how to do something
3 to practise for a competition or game

traitor someone who gives away a secret or gives information about his friends or country to the enemy

tramp 1 someone without a home or job who walks from place to place
2 to walk heavily

trample to spoil something by walking heavily on it

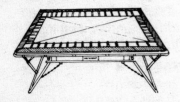

trampoline a large piece of canvas joined to a metal frame with springs for bouncing up and down on

trance a kind of sleep

transfer to move someone or something to another place
*He was **transferred** to a different team.*

transistor radio a kind of radio that you can carry about with you easily

transparent so clear that you can see through it. Glass is transparent.

transport to take people, animals, or things from one place to another

trap 1 something made for catching an animal and keeping it prisoner
2 to catch a person or animal by using a trap or a clever trick

trapdoor a kind of door in the floor or ceiling

trapeze a bar hanging from

ropes, used by acrobats

travel to go from one place to another

trawler a fishing boat that pulls a large net along the bottom of the sea

tray a flat piece of wood or tin used for carrying food, cups, plates, and other light things

treacherous not to be trusted
*The **treacherous** guard killed the king.*

treacle a thick, sweet, sticky liquid. Treacle is eaten on bread and used in making cakes and puddings.

tread (*rhymes with* bread) to walk on something
*He **trod** on his glasses and broke them.*
*They've **trodden** all over the daffodils.*

treason giving away your country's secrets to the enemy

treasure gold, silver, jewels, or other valuable things

treat 1 to behave towards someone or something in a certain way

*The horse had been badly **treated**.*

2 to pay for another person's food or drink
3 something special that pleases you very much
*a birthday **treat***

tree any tall plant with leaves, branches, and a thick stem of wood

tremble to shake because you are cold or frightened

tremendous very large or great
*a **tremendous** explosion*

trench a long, narrow hole dug in the ground

trespass to go on someone else's land, without asking him if you can

trial 1 trying something out to see how well it works
2 the time when a prisoner is in court. The people there decide whether or not he has done something wrong.

triangle a flat shape with three straight edges and three corners (see the list of shapes on page 248)

tribe a group of families who live together and are ruled by a chief

trick **1** something very clever that a person or animal has learnt to do
2 to make someone believe something that is not true

trickle to move like a very small stream of water

tricycle a machine with three wheels and two pedals that is ridden

tried see **try**

trifle cake and fruit covered in jelly, custard, and cream

trigger the part of a gun that is pulled to fire it

trim **1** to cut away the parts of something to make it neat and tidy
2 to decorate a piece of clothing
a coat **trimmed** *with fur*

trio a set of three people or things

trip **1** a short journey
a school **trip**
2 to fall over something
I **tripped** *over and broke my leg.*

triumphant very pleased because you have been successful
a **triumphant** *smile*

trod, trodden see **tread**

trolley **1** a small, narrow table on wheels
2 a kind of basket on wheels used in supermarkets

troop an organized group of soldiers or Scouts

tropical belonging to the very hot countries in Africa, Asia, and South America
tropical *plants*

trot one of the ways a horse can move. It is faster than a walk but slower than a canter.

trouble **1** something that upsets, worries, or bothers you
2 *to* **take trouble** *over something*
to take great care when you are doing something

trough (*say* troff) a long, narrow container that holds food or water for farm animals
a pig **trough**, *a horse* **trough**

trousers a piece of clothing that covers the body from the waist to the ankles and has separate parts for the legs
a pair of **trousers**

trout a fish found in rivers and lakes

trowel a small spade with a short handle

truant a pupil who stays away from school without permission

truck 1 a kind of lorry **2** a cart pulled by a railway engine, for carrying things

trudge to walk slowly and heavily because you are tired

true correct or real
a **true** story, a **true** friend

truly in a true or honest way

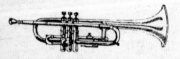

trumpet a brass musical instrument that is blown

trunk 1 a tree's thick stem **2** an elephant's long nose **3** a large box with a lid and handle for carrying things on a journey or storing things

trust to believe that someone or something will not let you down

truth something that is true

try 1 to work at something you want to be able to do **2** to test something
I **tried** it out before I bought it.

tub a round container
a **tub** of ice-cream

tube 1 a long, thin, round container
a **tube** of toothpaste
2 a long, thin, hollow piece of plastic, rubber, glass, or metal. Tubes are used for taking water and gas from one place to another.

tuck 1 to tidy away the loose ends of something
She **tucked** her blouse into her skirt.
2 tucked up warm and comfortable in bed

tuft a number of feathers, hairs, or blades of grass growing together

tug 1 to pull hard **2** a boat used for pulling ships

tulip a spring flower that grows from a bulb and is shaped like a cup

tumble to fall

tumbler a glass with a flat bottom
*a **tumbler** of water*

tune a series of notes that make a piece of music

tunic 1 a short dress worn over a skirt or trousers
2 a kind of long jacket worn as part of a uniform

tunnel a long hole that has been made under the ground or through a hill

turban a covering for the head made by wrapping cloth around it in a special way

turbine a kind of engine with a wheel inside it turned by gas, water, or steam

turf short grass and the soil it is growing in

turkey a large bird kept for its meat

turn 1 to move around

2 to change
*The prince **turned** into a frog.*
3 to become
*She **turned** pale.*
4 a time for you to do something that the others have done or are still waiting to do
*It's his **turn** to set the table.*

turnip a round, white vegetable eaten in the winter

turntable the part of a record-player that you put the record on

turpentine a kind of oil that can be used for cleaning paint brushes and mixed with paint to make it thinner

turret a small tower in a castle

turtle a sea creature that looks like a tortoise

tusk one of the two long, pointed teeth an elephant has

tweed warm cloth woven from wool
*a **tweed** coat*

tweezers a small tool for

getting hold of very thin things such as stamps
a pair of **tweezers**

twice two times

twig a small, thin branch

twilight the dim light at the end of the day before it gets completely dark

twin one of two children born to the same mother at the same time

twine thin, strong string

twinkle to shine with a lot of tiny flashes of bright light. Stars twinkle.

twirl to turn round and round quickly

twist **1** to turn or bend
a **twisted** *ankle*
2 to wrap things round each other

twitch to keep making quick movements with part of the body. Rabbits twitch their noses.

twitter to keep making quick, light sounds like a bird

type **1** one kind or sort
2 to write with a typewriter

typewriter a machine with keys that you press in order to print letters and numbers

tyre a circle of rubber round the rim of a wheel

Uu

ugly not pleasant to look at
the **ugly** *sisters*

umbrella a round piece of cloth stretched over a frame that can be opened and shut. You hold an umbrella over your head to keep off the rain.

umpire someone who makes sure that the rules are kept in games such as cricket and tennis

uncle your aunt's husband or the brother of one of your parents

uncomfortable not comfortable

unconscious (*say* un-kon-shuss)
in a very deep sleep
After the accident he was **unconscious** *for a week.*

under below

underground **1** under the ground
2 a railway that runs through

tunnels under the ground
*the London **Underground***

undergrowth bushes and other plants growing under tall trees

underline to draw a straight line underneath a word

underneath in a place under something

understand to know what something means or how it works
*He **understood** what the Frenchman said.*

underwear clothes made to be worn under other clothes

undo to open something that has been fastened with a knot or a button
*I **undid** the knot and opened the parcel.*
*Your shoe is **undone**.*

undress to take clothes off

uneven not smooth or level

unexpected not expected

unfair not right or just
*an **unfair** game*

ungrateful not grateful

unhappy not happy

unhealthy not healthy

unicorn an imaginary animal. It is like a horse, but has a

long, straight horn growing out of the front of its head.

uniform the special clothes that everyone in a group wears so that they look smart together
*a school **uniform***
*a policeman's **uniform***

union a group of workers who have joined together to make sure that everyone is treated fairly by the people in charge

unique very unusual because it is the only one of its kind
*a **unique** painting*

unit **1** the number one
*hundreds, tens, and **units***
2 an amount used in measuring or counting. Centimetres are units of length and pence are units of money.

unite to join together to make one

universal having to do with everyone and everything

universe all the worlds that there are and everyone and everything in them

university a place where some people go to study when they have left school

unkind not kind

unless if not

unlike not like

unload 1 to take off the things that an animal, boat, car, or lorry is carrying
They **unloaded** the ship at the dock.
2 to take the bullets out of a gun

unlock to open a door or box with a key

unlucky not lucky

unnecessary not necessary

unpleasant not pleasant

unruly badly behaved and difficult to control

untidy not tidy

until up to a certain time
I stayed up **until** midnight.

unusual not usual

unwell ill

unwrap to take something out

of the paper it is wrapped in

upon on or on top of

upper higher
the **upper** lip

upright 1 standing straight up
an **upright** post
2 honest
an **upright** person

uproar loud noise made by people who are angry or excited about something

upset 1 to make someone unhappy
2 to knock over
I **upset** the pot and spilt the paint.

upside-down turned over so that the bottom is at the top

upstairs the part of a house that you get to by climbing the stairs

upward, upwards moving to somewhere higher

urge 1 to try to make someone hurry to do something
2 a sudden, strong wish to do something

urgent so important that it needs to be answered or done at once
an **urgent** message
urgent work

use to do a job with something
I **used** paper and glue to make it.

useful **1** able to be used a lot
a **useful** tool
2 helpful
useful information

useless not useful

usual happening most often
Dinner is at the **usual** time.

utensil any tool, pot, or pan used in the kitchen

Vv

vacant with nobody in it
a **vacant** room

vaccination (say vak-si-nation)
an injection that stops you getting an illness

vacuum cleaner a machine that sucks up dust and dirt from floors and carpets

vague not clear or certain
a **vague** idea

vain **1** too proud of yourself and how you look
2 **in vain** without success

They tried **in vain** to save his life.

valley low land between hills

valuable worth a lot of money
valuable jewellery

value **1** the amount of money something could be sold for
2 how important or useful something is

valve a part in a machine that makes air, liquid, or electricity go in only one direction

vanilla the flavour that white ice-cream has

vanish to go away suddenly and not be seen any more

vanity being too proud of yourself

vapour steam, mist, or smoke

variety **1** a lot of different kinds of things
a **variety** of flavours
2 a certain sort

various different

varnish a clear liquid painted on to wood or metal to make it shiny

vary to be different
varied colours

vase a jar for holding flowers

vast very large

veal meat from a calf

vegetable part of a plant used as food. Vegetables are usually eaten with the main part of a meal.

vehicle anything that takes people or things from one place to another on land. Cars, vans, buses, bicycles, trains, carts, and lorries are all vehicles.

veil a piece of thin material used to cover the face or head

vein one of the narrow tubes inside the body, that carry blood to the heart

velvet thick material that is smooth and soft on one side
*a **velvet** dress*

venom the poison of snakes

ventilator a kind of opening in the wall of a room for letting in fresh air

veranda a long, open place with a roof built on to the side of a house

verb any of the words that tell you what someone or something is doing. *Come, go, sit, eat, sleep,* and *think* are all verbs.

verge grass growing along the edge of a road or path

verse part of a poem or song

version a story about something that has happened
*His **version** of the accident is different from mine.*

vertical upright

very most
*Ice is **very** cold.*

vessel **1** any container for liquid
2 a boat or ship

vest a piece of underwear worn on the top half of the body

vet someone whose job is to help animals that are ill or hurt to get better

vex to make someone angry

viaduct a long bridge that is a row of arches with a railway or road along the top of it

viaduct

vicar someone who serves God by being in charge of a church

vicious (*say* vish-uss) bad and cruel
a **vicious** kick, a **vicious** temper

victim someone who has been hurt, robbed, or killed

victory the winning of a fight or game

view **1** everything that can be seen from one place **2** what a person thinks about something

vigour strength

vile very nasty
a **vile** smell

village a group of houses together with a church and other buildings, in the country

villain a bad man

vine a plant that bunches of grapes grow on

vinegar a sour liquid put on food to make it taste better. People put salt and vinegar on chips.

violent very strong and rough
a **violent** storm

violet **1** a tiny purple or white flower that grows in spring **2** purple

violin a musical instrument made of wood with strings across it that are played with a bow

visibility how clearly something can be seen. In fog visibility is poor.

visible able to be seen

vision **1** the ability to see **2** a kind of dream

visitor someone who goes to see a person or place

vivid **1** bright
vivid colours
2 lively
a *vivid* imagination
3 so clear it seems real
a *vivid* dream

vixen a female fox

vocabulary a list of the words
someone uses

voice the sound you make
with your mouth when you
are speaking or singing

volcano a mountain that
contains hot liquid, gases,
and ash that sometimes
burst out of it
two *volcanoes*

volley several things shot or
thrown at the same time
a *volley* of bullets

volume **1** the amount of
space filled by something
2 one of a set of books
3 how loud a sound is

volunteer someone who
offers to do something that
he does not have to do

vote to say which person or
idea you think should be
chosen. Sometimes people
vote by putting up their
hands and sometimes by
making a mark on a piece of
paper.

voucher a printed paper you
can use instead of money for
buying certain things
a gift *voucher*

vow to make a serious
promise

vowel any one of the letters a,
e, i, o, u, and sometimes y

voyage a long journey by
boat

vulture a large bird that eats
dead animals

Ww

waddle to walk like a duck.
Ducks take very short steps
and move their bodies from
side to side.

wade to walk through water

wafer a very thin biscuit. Ice-cream often has wafers with it.

wag to move quickly from side to side
*The dog **wagged** its tail.*

wage, wages the money paid to someone for the job he does

wagon a cart with four wheels that is pulled by horses and used for moving heavy things

wail to make a long, sad cry

waist the narrow part in the middle of the body

waistcoat a short jacket without sleeves or a collar

wait to stay for something that you are expecting to happen

waiter a man who brings food to people in cafés, hotels, and restaurants

waitress a woman who brings food to people in cafés, hotels, and restaurants

wake to stop sleeping
***Wake** up!*
*He **woke** suddenly and saw the thief.*
*I was **woken** by the noise.*

walk to move along on foot

walkie-talkie a kind of radio that is carried about and can be used like a telephone

wall 1 a barrier made of bricks or stone put round a garden or field
2 one of the sides of a building or room

wallet a small, flat, leather case for pound notes and papers that is carried in the pocket

walnut a kind of nut with a hard shell

waltz a kind of dance done with a partner

wand a thin stick used for casting magic spells. In stories fairies and wizards have wands.

wander to move about without trying to get anywhere

want **1** to feel that you would like to have something **2** to need

war a fight between countries

ward a bedroom for patients in a hospital

wardrobe a cupboard where clothes are hung

warehouse a large building in which things are stored

wares things that are on sale

warm fairly hot
a **warm** room

warn to tell someone that he is in danger

warren an area of ground where a lot of rabbits live

warrior someone fighting in a battle

wart a dry, hard spot on the skin

wash to make something clean with water

washing clothes that need washing or are being washed

washing-machine a machine that washes clothes

wasp an insect that flies and can sting

waste **1** to use more of something than you need to **2** things that you get rid of because you do not need them any more
waste paper

watch **1** to look at **2** a small clock that is worn or carried

watchman someone whose job is to guard a building at night

water the clear liquid in rivers and seas. It falls from the sky as rain.

waterfall a stream of water falling from a high place to a low place

waterproof made of material that does not let water through
a **waterproof** coat

watertight made so that water cannot get into it
watertight boots

waves **1** one of the lines of water you can see moving on the surface of the sea **2** to move your hand to say hello or goodbye to someone

*Look, she's **waving** to you.*
3 to move up and down or from side to side

wavy with curves in it
* **wavy** hair, a **wavy** line*

wax something that melts very easily and is used for making candles, crayons, and polish. Some wax is made by bees and some is made from oil.

way **1** a road or path
2 how something is done

weak not strong
*a **weak** person, **weak** tea*

weaken **1** to get weaker
2 to make weaker

wealth a lot of money or treasure

wealthy rich

weapon something used to hurt another person in a fight

wear **1** to be dressed in something
*I **wore** that dress last time.*
2 to wear out to become weak and useless because it has been used so much
3 to wear someone out to make someone very tired
*He was **worn out** after the match.*

weary very tired

weasel a small, furry animal with a long body. It kills and eats mice, rats, and rabbits.

weather rain, snow, ice, fog, wind, and sun

weave to make material by pushing a thread under and over other threads
*She made a loom and **wove** a scarf on it.*
*The bag was **woven** in straw.*

web a thin, sticky net spun by a spider to trap insects

web-foot a foot with its toes joined together by skin. Ducks, otters, and other animals that swim a lot have web-feet.

wedding the time when a man and woman get married

wedge **1** a piece that is thick at one end and thin at the other like a triangle or the letter V
*a **wedge** of cake*
2 to keep two things apart by

pushing something between them

weed any wild plant that grows where it is not wanted

week the seven days from Sunday to the next Saturday

weekend Saturday and Sunday

weep to let tears fall from the eyes
*He **wept** because he was lost.*

weigh **1** to find the weight of something
2 to have a certain weight

weight **1** how heavy something is
2 a round piece of metal put on the scales when something is being weighed

weird (*rhymes with* beard) very strange

welcome to show that you are pleased when someone or something arrives

welfare the health and happiness of people

well **1** healthy
2 in a good way
*He swims **well**.*
3 a hole dug to get water or oil out of the ground

wellingtons rubber boots

that keep the feet and part of the legs dry
*a pair of **wellingtons***

went see **go**

wept see **weep**

west in the direction of the setting sun

western **1** from the west or in the west
2 a cowboy film

whack to hit hard with a stick

whale the largest sea animal there is

wharf a place where ships are loaded and unloaded

what **1** which thing
***What** is that?*
2 that which
*Tell me **what** you think.*

whatever no matter what
***Whatever** happens, I'll help you.*

wheat a plant grown by farmers. Its seed is used for making flour.

wheel **1** a circle of wood or metal fixed in the middle so that it can keep turning round. Cars, bicycles, carts, and some machines have wheels.
2 to push a bicycle, pram, or cart

wheelbarrow a small cart with one wheel at the front, that is pushed

when **1** at what time
When are you coming?
2 at the time that
When I moved, it flew away.

whenever at any time

where in what place
Where are you?

wherever no matter where
Wherever you are, I'll find you.

whether if
She asked *whether* I could come.

which what person or thing
Which do you want?

while in the time that something else is happening
He fell asleep *while* the television was on.

whimper the soft sound an animal makes when it is frightened or hurt

whine the long, sad sound a dog makes when it is unhappy

whip **1** a long piece of rope or leather joined to a handle and used for hitting things
2 to stir cream hard to make it thick
whipped cream

whirl to turn round and round very quickly

whisk **1** to move very quickly
2 to stir hard

whisker a strong hair that grows on the faces of men and animals. A cat has long whiskers growing at each side of its mouth.

whisky a very strong drink made from corn or potatoes

whisper to speak very softly

whistle **1** to make a shrill sound by blowing through the lips
2 something that makes a shrill sound when it is blown

Whit Sunday the seventh Sunday after Easter. It is also called **Whitsun**.

who what person
Who did that?

whoever no matter what person
Whoever did it will be in trouble.

whole **1** not broken
Swallow it **whole**.
2 all of something
the **whole** *world*

whooping-cough (*say*
hooping cough)
an illness that makes you
keep coughing and breathing
in heavily

whose belonging to what
person
Whose *is this?*

why because of what
Why *did you do that?*

wick the string that goes
through the middle of a
candle

wicked very bad
a **wicked** *witch*

wicket the set of three stumps
with two bails on top of them
in cricket (see **bail** and
stump)

wide **1** measuring a lot from
one side to the other
2 completely
wide *awake,* **wide** *open*

widow a woman whose
husband has died

widower a man whose wife
has died

width how wide something is

wife a woman married to
someone.
Henry VIII had six **wives**.

wig a covering of false hair
worn on the head

wigwam the kind of tent
American Indians lived in

wild **1** not looked after by
people
a **wild** *flower*
2 not controlled
a **wild** *horse, a* **wild** *temper*

wilderness wild land where
no one lives

wilful wanting to do
something, even though
other people say it is wrong
a **wilful** *child*

will **1** a kind of letter left by a
dead person. It tells people
what he wants to be done
with his money and things.
2 the power to choose what
you want to do
3 is going to
He **will** *be nine tomorrow.*

We'll soon be there.
*I said I **would** be late.*
I'd like another cake.

willing ready and happy to do what is wanted

willow a kind of tree that grows near water and has thin branches that bend easily. Its wood is used for making cricket bats.

wily crafty
*a **wily** fox*

win 1 to get a prize
2 to beat someone else in a game or fight
*We've **won** four matches and lost two.*

wince to move slightly because you are upset or in pain

wind¹ (*rhymes with* grinned) air moving along quickly

wind² (*rhymes with* blind)
1 to turn a key to make a machine work
*The clock started when she **wound** it up.*
2 to wrap cloth, thread, tape, or string tightly round something

windmill a mill that uses wind to make its machinery work. It has four blades fixed to it

in the shape of a cross and the wind makes these turn.

window an opening in the wall of a building. It is filled with glass and lets in light.

wine a strong drink made from grapes

wing one of the parts of a bird or insect used for flying
*a pair of **wings***

wink to close and open one eye quickly

winter the coldest part of the year

wipe to rub something with a cloth to dry it or clean it

wire a long, thin strip of metal that can be bent into different shapes

wireless a radio

wisdom the ability to understand many things

wise able to understand many things

wish to say or think what you would like to happen

wisp a little bit of straw, hair, or smoke

witch a woman who uses magic to do bad things. Witches in fairy stories have tall, black, pointed hats and ride in the air on brooms.

with **1** having
a man **with** *a wooden leg*
2 in the company of
I came **with** *a friend.*
3 using
It was written **with** *a pen.*
4 against
fighting **with** *the enemy*

wither to dry up and get paler and smaller
withered *flowers*

without not having
without *any money*

witness someone who sees something important happen

witty clever and funny

wives more than one **wife**

wizard a man in fairy stories, who can do magic things

wobble to shake or rock. Jelly wobbles.

woke, woken see **wake**

wolf a wild animal like a big, fierce dog
a pack of **wolves**

woman a fully grown female
The three **women** *were sisters.*

won see **win**

wonder **1** a feeling of surprise because of something strange or marvellous
2 to ask yourself about something
I **wonder** *who did it.*

wonderful so good that it surprises you
a **wonderful** *holiday*

wood **1** the branches and trunks of trees cut up so that they can be used for making things or burnt on fires
2 a lot of trees growing together

wooden made of wood

woodpecker a bird that eats insects living in tree trunks. It has a strong beak for making holes in wood and a long, sticky tongue for catching insects.

woodwork making things out of wood
*a **woodwork** lesson*

wool the thick, soft hair that covers sheep. It is spun into thread and used for making cloth and for knitting.

woollen made of wool

word a sound or group of sounds that means something when you say it, write it, or read it

wore see **wear**

work a job or something else that you have to do

workman a man paid to work with his hands, a tool, or a machine

workshop a place where things are made or mended

world the earth or anything else in space that is like it

worm a long, thin creature that wriggles about in the soil

worn see **wear**

worry **1** to be upset because you are thinking about something bad that might happen
2 to get hold of something with the teeth and shake it, as dogs do with slippers

worse less good
*He's a **worse** swimmer than I am.*

worship to love and praise God

worst least good
*He's the **worst** in the class at swimming.*

worth with a certain value
*This old stamp is **worth** £100.*

worthless not worth anything

would see **will**

wound¹ (*say* woond) an injury from something like a knife or a bullet

wound² (*rhymes with* sound) see **wind²**

243

wove, woven see **weave**

wrap to put cloth or paper round something

wrath (*say* roth) anger

wreath flowers or leaves twisted together into a ring
a holly **wreath**

wreck **1** to damage a ship, building, or car so badly that it cannot be used again
2 a ship, building, or car so badly damaged that it cannot be used again

wren a very small, brown bird

wrestle to struggle with someone

wretched (*say* retch-id)
1 unhappy or ill
2 poor
wretched *health*

wriggle to twist and turn the body about like a worm

wring to squeeze and twist something wet to get the water out of it
She washed the towel and **wrung** *it.*

wrinkle a small crease in the skin. Old people usually have a lot of wrinkles.

wrist the thin part of the arm where it is joined to the hand

write to put words or signs on paper so that people can read them
I **wrote** *to her last week. You have* **written** *this very neatly.*

writhe to twist or roll about because you are in great pain

writing something that has been written
untidy **writing**
a piece of **writing**

written see **write**

wrong not right
the **wrong** *answer*

wrote see **write**

wrung see **wring**

Xx

X-ray a special photograph that shows the inside of a body so that doctors can see if there is anything wrong

xylophone a row of wooden bars that you hit with small

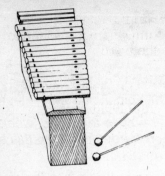

hammers to make musical sounds

Yy

yacht (*say* yot)

a light boat with sails, used for racing

yard **1** a measure for length

2 ground that is next to a building and has a wall round it

yawn to open your mouth wide because you are tired

year a measure for time. A year is twelve months or three hundred and sixty-five days.

yell to shout

yelp to give a quick, shrill cry like a dog in pain

yesterday the day before today

yew a kind of tree that has dark green leaves it keeps all through the year

yield **1** to give in
*The fort **yielded** to the enemy.*
2 the amount of fruit or grain on a plant
*a good **yield** of apples*

yodel to shout with a musical sound, changing from a low note to a high note and back again

yoghurt a thick liquid made from sour milk. It usually has fruit in it and you eat it with a spoon.

yoke a long, curved piece of wood joined to a cart. It is

Zz

zebra an animal like a horse with black and white stripes. Zebras are found in Africa.

zero the number nothing, also written 0

zig-zag a line with sudden turns in it like this

zip, zipper a special fastener for joining two edges of material together. Some dresses, trousers, and bags have zips.

zone a part of a town, country, or the world that is special in some way
a parking **zone**

zoo a place where different kinds of wild animals are kept so that people can go and see them

zoom to move very quickly

put over the necks of two oxen to help them pull the cart.

yolk (*rhymes with* joke) the round, yellow part of an egg

you the person or people you are speaking to
You *are reading these words.*

young born not long ago. A kitten is a young cat.

youngster someone who is young

your belonging to you
your *book*

yourself, yourselves
1 you and no one else
2 *by yourself, by yourselves* on your own

youth **1** a boy or young man
2 the time in your life when you are young

Numbers

1	one	first
2	two	second
3	three	third
4	four	fourth
5	five	fifth
6	six	sixth
7	seven	seventh
8	eight	eighth
9	nine	ninth
10	ten	tenth
11	eleven	eleventh
12	twelve	twelfth
13	thirteen	thirteenth
14	fourteen	fourteenth
15	fifteen	fifteenth
16	sixteen	sixteenth
17	seventeen	seventeenth
18	eighteen	eighteenth
19	nineteen	nineteenth
20	twenty	twentieth
21	twenty-one	twenty-first
22	twenty-two	twenty-second
30	thirty	thirtieth
40	forty	fortieth
50	fifty	fiftieth
60	sixty	sixtieth
70	seventy	seventieth
80	eighty	eightieth
90	ninety	ninetieth
100	a hundred	hundredth
101	a hundred and one	hundred and first
200	two hundred	two hundredth
1,000	a thousand	thousandth
1,000,000	a million	millionth

Flat shapes

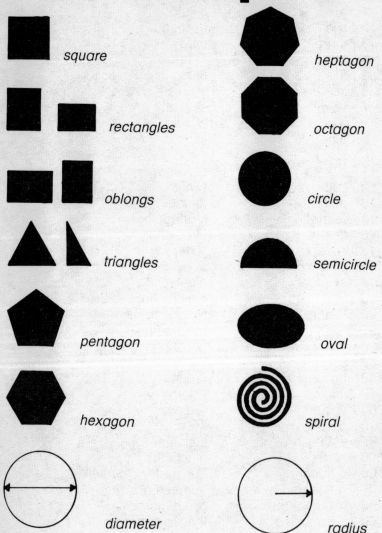

square

rectangles

oblongs

triangles

pentagon

hexagon

heptagon

octagon

circle

semicircle

oval

spiral

diameter

radius

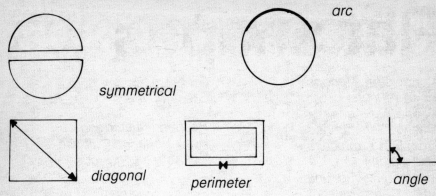

symmetrical

arc

diagonal

perimeter

angle

Solid shapes

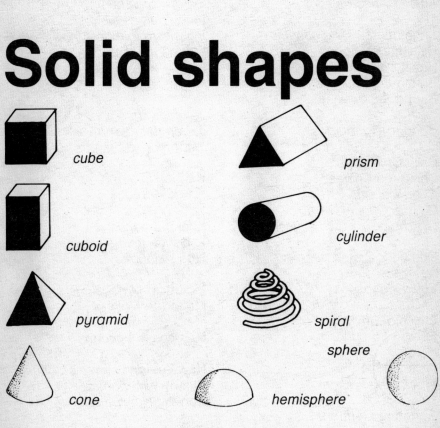

cube

prism

cuboid

cylinder

pyramid

spiral

sphere

cone

hemisphere

Places Peoples

Afghanistan *Afghans*
Africa *Africans*
Algeria *Algerians*
America *Americans*
Argentina *Argentinians*
Asia *Asians*
Australia *Australians*
Austria *Austrians*

Bangladesh *Bangladeshis*
Belgium *Belgians*
Brazil *Brazilians*
Britain *the British*
Burma *the Burmese*

Canada *Canadians*
Ceylon *see* Sri Lanka
Chile *Chileans*
China *the Chinese*
Cuba *Cubans*
Cyprus *Cypriots*
Czechoslovakia *Czechoslovaks*

Denmark *Danes*

Egypt *Egyptians*
England *the English*
Ethiopia *Ethiopians*
Europe *Europeans*

Finland *Finns*
France *the French*

Germany *Germans*
Ghana *Ghanaians*

Great Britain *see* Britain
Greece *Greeks*

Holland *the Dutch*
Hong Kong *the Chinese*
Hungary *Hungarians*

Iceland *Icelanders*
India *Indians*
Indonesia *Indonesians*
Ireland *the Irish*
Israel *Israelis*
Italy *Italians*

Jamaica *Jamaicans*
Japan *the Japanese*
Jordan *Jordanians*

Kenya *Kenyans*
Korea *Koreans*

Lapland *Lapps*
Lebanon *the Lebanese*
Libya *Libyans*

Malaysia *Malaysians*
Malta *the Maltese*
Mexico *Mexicans*
Morocco *Moroccans*

New Zealand *New Zealanders*
Nigeria *Nigerians*
Norway *Norwegians*

Pakistan *Pakistanis*

Poland *Poles*
Portugal *the Portuguese*

Russia *Russians*

Saudi Arabia *Saudis*
Scotland *Scots*
Spain *Spaniards*
Sri Lanka *the Sinhalese*
Sweden *Swedes*
Switzerland *the Swiss*
Syria *Syrians*

Tanzania *Tanzanians*
Thailand *Thais*
Trinidad *Trinidadians*

Turkey *Turks*

Uganda *Ugandans*
United Kingdom *see* Britain
United States (USA) *Americans*

Venezuela *Venezuelans*
Vietnam *the Vietnamese*

Wales *the Welsh*
West Indies *West Indians*

Yugoslavia *Yugoslavs*

Zambia *Zambians*
Zimbabwe *Zimbabweans*

Continents

Africa
Antarctica
Asia
Australia

Europe
North America
South America

Planets

Mercury
Venus
Earth
Mars
Jupiter

Saturn
Uranus
Neptune
Pluto

Days

Sunday
Monday
Tuesday
Wednesday

Thursday
Friday
Saturday

Months

January
February
March
April
May
June

July
August
September
October
November
December

Colours

beige
black
blue
brown
cream
crimson
fawn
green
grey
indigo
lavender
lemon

lilac
maroon
orange
pink
purple
red
scarlet
turquoise
violet
white
yellow